GRANTASMS

TWISTED WORDS FOR COMMUNICATION FUN

GRANT ALLEN CROWELL

ONE TWISTED SQUIRREL, LLC

TABLE OF MALCONTENTS

First paperback edition, November 2019

Published in Durham, North Carolina by One Twisted Squirrel, LLC.

Book design by Grant Crowell. Front book cover design features stock image attributed to ©iliveinoctober/DepositPhotos.com

ISBN 978-0-578-52346-0

Library of Congress Control Number: 2019907868

Printed in the United States of America. Well, ask Amazon.com, I didn't really check on that. But it sounds cool and patriotic, yah?

Praise for Grantasms

"This book is Grantastic! And I KNOW books! You'll laugh. You'll cry. You'll think. It's that good!"

~*Douglas Burdett, Host of The Marketing Book Podcast— named by LinkedIn as one of " 10 Podcasts That Will Make You a Better Marketer" and by Forbes as one of " 11 Podcasts That Will Keep You In The Know."*

"Grant Crowell is a master at articulating what nearly everyone is scared to say out loud. He comes up with signature phrases about the funny acts our minds and bodies do like no one else does. Mark my words—you'll remember, use, and share these Grantasms with friends, foes and family. (There's probably some overlap in there.)"

~*Alice Osborn, author/poet/musician.*

"This book speaks the language we've all been waiting for! Grantasms is simply another creative way of what I call "speaking human." Because the more human you are, the more you will stand out and build a level of trust that's unbreakable. Buy this book and you'll discover what it means to be fully human!"

~*Bryan Kramer, Keynote & TED Speaker, Business Coach, Forbes Columnist, and Best-Selling Author of "There is no more B2B or B2C. It's H2H: Human to Human."*

"This book will ignite your hidden creative side waiting to be set free and express your unique words of meaning, purpose, and humor. These words will become your unique language with the people you communicate with every day! You will find yourself constantly referring to the various examples and effective strategies in Grant's book. Grantasms will help you develop the skills to formulate words that are genuinely yours. Words that will make you feel good creating and communicating a different, practical language in an amusing, fun, and memorable manner."

~David Giwerc, Founder & President, ADD Coach Academy, MCAC, MCC; Author of "Permission to Proceed, The Keys to Creating a Life Full of Passion, Purpose and Possibility for Adults with ADHD."

In the interests of transparency, here now are some *highly critical* reviews of this book...

"I'm not saying that this is the worst book ever, only because I want to gouge my eyes out and I've lost the will to read another book after this horrible experience."

"Human rights groups are already declaring this book a torture technique."

"I wondered why my ears are bleeding. Now I know."

"Maybe someone should buy a hundred copies of this. It makes a good fire starter for camping."

~Karen Mueller, Grant's live-in partner.

What the fun are Grantasms?

GRANTASMS (gran-taz-ums) *n.*

TWISTED WORDS WITH GENUINE STORIES FOR
ENJOYABLE CONNECTIONS

Grantasms are the names I give to my comic and meaningful word creations for our "social era." I create them for laughs, personal growth, and creative inspiration. They're inspired by my own true stories, and they help me better connect and converse with people everywhere. They also playfully encourage others to do the same.

I LOVE MAKING UP AND SHARING WORDS

Well, maybe I should let someone else explain, someone who knows me pretty well and whom I'll be referring to semi-regularly through this book, my partner Karen.

"Grant makes shit up all day. No one pays for it, but it makes him happy. He prefers it over doing work."

OK, maybe that wasn't the best testimonial choice if I'm going to sell any books.

Like a little taste test before you dig deep? Enjoy a sneak preview feast of these delicious word tater tots with some snack-size micro-stories. And, if you want, imagine me wearing a tall, poofy, twisted word chef hat while serving them to you.

---

aisle anger (i ul an gur) *n.*
The feeling of road rage when stuck behind oblivious people in a grocery store.

I'm overcome with aisle anger when I'm right behind a shopper who stops to check something out while having their cart turned sideways, blocking my path while they jabber on their phone. Of course, this person gets annoyed when I interrupt their conversation, asking them to please move to the side. Maybe they need an "aisle anger-management" class.

---

beditating (bed eh tay teen) *v.*
Meditating while lying down rather than with a straight, upright back.

Meditation purists say that beditating isn't the "correct" way because it will make your meditation sessions sleepy. However, many people in my meditating Facebook group swear that being able to lie down while meditating is soooo relaxing. Plus, what about pregnant women when their belly doesn't allow them to sit up straight? Beditate it!

flabs (flabz) *n.*
What a formerly in-shape person now calls their abs.

Even though I won't ever get the ripped look, my flabs still have the six-pack underneath. I'm just showing a kegger on the surface.

hex (hex) *n.*
An ex who makes your life so terrible that you believe you're cursed.

I had a hex who keyed my car with a long scratch all the way across my doors and insulted me to my clients. She then texted me a week later for a booty call.

ice-crusher (eyes kruh shur) *v.*
An icebreaker that succeeds amazingly with your intended conversation partner.

I love it when I have an ice-crusher so that I'll be well-remembered after the party's over.

Good signs that I've "ice-crushed" include: my intended audience laughing out loud at one of my Grantasms, listening intently to the story behind it, sharing relatable stories of their own, and finding inspiration to share their own words. Or sometimes, it's just letting others share their own story without interrupting.

(However, if the person is very long-winded and making others uncomfortable, you can "ice-crush" it by knowing when to interject and turn the conversation to something else.)

---

menopaucalypse (men o paw ca lips) *n.*
When you experience menopause so bad that it makes you lose your internal filter, your job, and your money.

You should talk to my hex about that.

---

multicrashing (mull tee cra sheen) *n.*
When you physically collide with someone because you're distracted by a digital device.

I like to listen to podcasts when I'm running. One time, I had started my cool-down with fast walking in my townhome subdivision. I was looking down at the sidewalk as I typed notes into my phone app from the episode I had just heard.

BANG! I bumped into a full-figured, blonde-haired woman in a blue jogging shirt. She'd done the same thing! We were two people, too occupied with multitasking to pay attention to what was right in front of us. We laughed about it together, and became friendly neighbors with a funny story of how we first met, by nearly multicrashing.

---

relationshit (ree lay shun shit) *n.*

What you call someone to whom you've been a good partner or friend, but they grossly neglect the friendship after they've received help from you in their own time of need.

I once supported a friend for many months before, during, and after her medical treatment. She needed someone to talk to and help her get around, which was indeed understandable. She confided in me during this time of how depressed she'd get, how her boss made her feel terrible, how her kids were struggling and her struggles with parenting them. I tried to be a good friend and offer a helping hand and moral support. Fortunately, her treatment was a success.

However, after she was all well, she blew me off completely—for months.

One day, out of the blue, she texted me a link she said reminded her of me. So I offered one more time to meet for coffee, but she refused and said she wanted a digital pen-pal friendship only— no explanation.

Boy, what a relationshit. (Thanks at least for giving me inspiration for the word and the story, though!)

HEALING WITH HUMOR

Grantasms are good for laughs, but there's more to it. I discovered after many years of creating and sharing my twisted words that there are some amazing socio-emotional health benefits as well.

As you can see from my last word example, I sometimes need therapeutic humor to get over a bad experience. Or at least, to find the humor in it and grow as a person. If you've been struggling with something that's been getting you down (and you want to get yourself back up and move on), Grantasms help you learn to laugh at your mistakes and failures.

How, exactly? **By giving them fun names which others can relate to.**

I've found that when you can address something with a positive mindset, you're more likely to forgive yourself and tackle them with success the next time they're bound to happen. Plus, you help others from your triumphs and shared struggles. They are your "healing with humor."

CREATIVE COMMUNICATION

I like to say my Grantasms are "word fungasms" or **"wordgasms."** Because they're mine or the stories are mine, I use my first name given to me by my parents, "Grant," to share my connection to the words with others. They help me express myself better when existing words in our standard dictionaries fail me. They really are stress-free (and stress-relieving) creativity for even the most unfamiliar and awkward situations, which make me appear confident and charismatic in mixed social company. Like I mentioned earlier, they're more than fun icebreakers; they're "ice-crushers!"

PLAYFUL MINDFULNESS

I "Grantasm" regularly to improve my emotional intelligence, working memory, social skills, and to get outside my own comfort zone. Through them, I've learned to flip anxiety into creativity, boredom into a brain game, distractions into directions, and icebreakers into warm relationships.

LAUGH AND LEARN

I'm sharing with you all my favorite words and secrets behind these Grantasms so you can quickly and easily laugh while learning, and it never feels like work. I also refer to this part as "sassy self-help."

QUIRKY EMPATHY

Many of these Grantasms are tongue-in-cheek, but I also create them for human connection—a social bond through a funny, shared experience. Through them, I discover we're all unique and yet not all that different. The more I create and share them, the more I learn about other people and myself, and how we're connected—including with people I wouldn't otherwise ever think to have *anything* in common!

VERSATILE VERBOSITY

This book has Grantasms for all kinds of social situations—from the mundane to the insane, and everywhere in-between. You can relate to them, use them for your own stories, and find the creative inspiration to invent your own words.

DISTRACTIONS INTO DIRECTIONS

Grantasms helped me manage my ADHD, and taught me how to use it to help others. It doesn't matter whether or not you've been diagnosed with ADHD, ADD, or a similar neurocognitive condition. As long as you have good intentions, Grantasms help you calm and coordinate your wandering *a-tension*. They actually make focus, fun!

WHAT'S IN THIS BOOK?

A nine-course feast, that's what! *Yessirree* (and yes ma'am, and yes gender non-binaries), each Grantasms word chapter has its own twisted theme, all for your reading pleasure and social word culinary delight.

1. **Words At Play | Grantasms for Everyday—**
   Enjoy a warm-up round, because some words are just fun to say (and come up with).
2. **Gimmee Money | Grantasms for Work—**
   Stupid jobs and the short end of the money stick. Terrible bosses and unethical companies are no longer safe.
3. **Yay for Food | Grantasms for Eats—**
   Encouragement to play with your food. Made-up words for food also make savory syllabic experiences. Or, they can salvage a bad experience from whatever you put in your mouth, and whatever comes out of it.
4. **OKStupid | Grantasms for Relationshits—**
   Funny moments and *faux pas* with dating-mating and relation-shipwrecks. If you ever grimaced because you just got hit on online by a coworker who looks like one of your parents, now you can laugh about it openly.

5. **ADHDelirious | Grantasms for Distractions**—All strange things about Attention Deficit Hyperactivity Disorder—because I got ADHD—oh so bad, oh so good.

6. **Digital Douches | Grantasms for Interwebz**—Big and little online screw-ups to laugh about, and what righteously (and self-righteously) pisses us off. Now you have the perfect retort for the jerk who makes a friend request on Facebook and then spams you with multi-level-marketing products.

7. **Super Socialize Me | Grantasms for Gerks**—Geeks, nerds, and dorks dedicated to improving their social skills and becoming amazing citizens.

8. **Farty Party | Grantasms for Poof**—Because there's more than just one name for a fart than "fart" and "FARRRRRTTTTTTT!!!!" If you have never made up a fart name in your life, now's the time to bust out the creative gasses and let 'em rip.

9. **Oops Poops | Grantasms for #2**—Everybody poops, including Jesus and the Pope. I bet they both came up with names for poop as well. ("Holy shit" may have been one of them.)

LET'S FEAST ON MULTIPLE GRANTASMS!

PARTO UNO
(GRANTASMS FOR FUN)

Words at play!
Grantasms for everyday

"Play is the joy of being fully present and engaged without fear of failure, a pleasant venture into the unknown."

~DANA KELLER, PLAY ADVOCATE

Twisted words can be just for play. No agenda, no objective—simply have fun. Wordplay with yourself all day long if you like, you won't get sore!

Social wordplay for me is way more fun than regular wordplay. Grantasms don't require a partner, but they are great to share *with* a partner, any partner—even an unsuspecting one (with good intentions, of course).

Play is what breaks the ice into a good, stiff word cocktail time. Consider this your fun, guilt-free warm-up!

---

alt-winning (alt win een) *v.*
A positive spin on losing.

Alt-winning can be delusional when it's what people say when they are too afraid to admit failure. "Hey, honey, I didn't lose all of our money at the casino. I was alt-winning!"

hyposexual (hip oh sex shu all) *adj.*
The private (or not-so-private) sexual behavior of a politician that grossly deviates from their public positions, i.e., a sexual hypocrite.

Who are some hyposexuals that come to mind? How about the staunch pro-life politician caught pressuring his mistress to get an abortion? Or, a guy who does LGBTQ conversion therapy and get caught at a gay massage parlor?

---

meditargeting (meh de tar guh teen) *n.*
Meditating while waiting for your significant other to finish shopping at Target.

I've caught myself meditargeting against the back store wall with my eyes closed while doing deep-breathing exercises.

---

oopsie-owee (oop cee ow whee) *n.*

Doing something klutzy and ended up hurting yourself.

Yeah, me too, like a thousand times. I remember one time I gave myself a huge oopsie-owee, and I'm still suffering from it today. I was running through a supermarket parking lot and I tripped over the pavement—SPLAT! POP! Boy, did I come down hard, right on my already-hurting tennis elbow, swelling further to the size of a baseball. For weeks I couldn't even push down on a shampoo bottle without an assist.

At least I didn't injure myself while on the toilet. That would have been a poopsie-owee.

---

phockets (fah kitz) *n.*
Phony pockets sewn shut on the inside of clothing, so you can't put anything in them.

You're supposed to un-stitch them if you want, but why go through the effort? Phuckit. Phockets also apply to pants where the pockets are so short that nothing you put in them will stay inside. Whoever are the perpetrators of this annoyingly useless fashion accessory, I say, "phock you!"

---

purplefect (purr pull fect) *n.*
The perfect version of purple, or when purple is the solution.

Purple is my favorite color. Not only is it symbolic of creativity, but was also the color I needed for my wallet and my iPhone, so I don't keep losing them.

It'd be even more purplefect if I could find a cool purple iPhone cover for men that also doubles as a wallet, so I wouldn't need to carry around two items with me. Currently I have a brown suede one, which is purple-free-fect, I guess. (Well, I have a purple coffee-cup holder, at least.)

---

sippie (sih pee) *n.*
A progressive-leaning northerner who's moved, or "slipped" down to the south.

My partner and I moved from the Chicago burbs to the Raleigh-Durham area of North Carolina, which is considered to be one of the more progressive parts of the state. Our current residence is so inundated with northern transplants that I like to refer to it as sippie-town. We take the best parts of local southern culture and mix it with our own.

**GRANTASMS ARE YOUR WORDGASMS FOR
PLAY, EVERY DAY!**

Gimmee money! Grantasms for work

"Happiness is not in the mere possession of money; it lies in the joy of achievement, in the thrill of creative effort."

~FRANKLIN D. ROOSEVELT, 20TH CENTURY AMERICAN PRESIDENT

"Words are the money of fools."

~THOMAS HOBBES, 17TH CENTURY BRITISH PHILOSOPHER

I've certainly been a fool with my desire and need for money—as a consumer, employee, freelancer, entrepreneur, and relationship opportunist. What do I count as wins? Using my combination of original words and social skills to make something financially pleasant happen, or lessening the blow of a financial setback.

I've had remarkable highs and lows with dough. Growing up in Hawai'i, I worked far too long on "fun" jobs that owners stiff you on because they think you love to work for them for next to nothing. In my adulthood, I got an inheritance from the passing of my parents and blew much of it on a documentary video dream I had, with no clear business plan. (I did at least manage to save many choice clips on my YouTube channel.)

I had an online marketing business for ten years and went bankrupt with the 2008 recession. Everyone was late on payments, or decided to just stop paying on bills due to me, or even try to sue me to get their money back (while keeping all the deliverables).

Oh yeah, and I also sucked at running a business.

Eventually I ran out of cash and had creditors calling me non-stop. My anxiety was so high that I was having night sweats frequently, and I procrastinated on filing tax returns for several years—YEARS! I also hadn't kept a salaried job for longer than a year for 13 years. (Yeah, some prize I was, right?)

I'm incredibly fortunate to have found a life partner who changed my behavior and got me not only to stay debt-free but with savings and retirement accounts of my own. I now have a credit rating that hovers on the high of "very good," and I one day hope to get it to "excellent."

"Wealth is the ability to fully experience life."

~HENRY DAVID THOREAU

Today I consider myself wealthy, not in the traditional sense of many zeros in a bank account, but as in having an abundance of something I treasure: my social-emotional health and human connections. Of course, I still want the things that most others want—financial security. I.e., a steady income with passive income streams as a backup, investments that yield higher returns, a nest egg, and a safety net. Why can't I have it all?

Oh yeah, I have to be more focused and disciplined, first.

"Money is not the only answer, but it makes a difference."

~BARACK OBAMA

Finances stress a lot of us more than they should. Coming up with Grantasms help me ease the natural stress most of us have about making a living. Making up these words reminds me to laugh, relax, and better deal with money-matters.

That said, I wouldn't mind having more money. Gimmee some!

---

acronumb (ak ro num) *adj.*
Going numb from having to process way too many acronyms.

"What is the NPP with our PP for setting up SSO TBC by COB?" I have to fight off acronumb-ness sometimes at contract gigs where clients have their corporate-speak. I almost feel the need to have a language interpreter while I hunt down the meanings for all of those abbreviations, which often delves into acrononsense.

bettersweet (beh tur sweet) *adj.*

A job you get hired for, only because you happened to be available after getting fired from, or quitting, your previous employment.

It was bettersweet when I got terminated from a job when I refused the CEO/founder's order to do sketchy stuff. I had only been working there a short time, and it caused significant issues finding my next job.

I did eventually land another position elsewhere. I managed to stay there long enough to land a contract gig with an international tech firm and resign from my old job on good terms. My pay is now way better, my colleagues are more professional, and I get to work remote. I guess you could call that "bettersweeter."

bitterview (bih tur vyou) *n.*

A job interview you realize early on that it's going to be a complete waste of your eff-ing time.

I remember a job interview where I filled out multiple application forms and a personality test that took a couple of hours, ended up waiting another hour, and finally sitting in a room with three people who barely managed eye contact.

I'd be peppered with pointless questions such as "Where do you see yourself five years from now?" (That was asked to me by a guy that had quit his previous job after eighteen months; I checked on LinkedIn!)

It was evident to me that my interview was just a formality when they didn't even bother to shake my hand on the way out. I felt a little bitter then, but not so much to write them up a negative review on Glassdoor.

---

breadcrummer (bred cru mur) *n.*
Someone who is not the primary breadwinner but still contributes, somewhat.

When I was the breadcrummer in our relationship, I had to learn how to spend my time more wisely. I was dealing with a significant decrease in pay, along with no paid days off and no benefits. I made sure I was contributing in other ways besides financially, such as helping more around the house, spending time with my partner, and just committing to getting my book done. So, even when I was the breadcrummer, I didn't feel too breadcrummy.

---

business discard (biz niz diss card) *v.*
A business card you already know you'll be getting rid of.

Many business cards that people offer me at networking events are business discards. They're passed out like cheap candy, usually from sketchy sales or marketing folks, or just lazy entrepreneurs with poor social skills who can't be bothered with genuine conversation. Somehow they consider exchanging business cards as permission to put me on their automated email list.

---

entrypreneur (in tree pre nuer) *n.*

1. A new entrepreneur who has a lot to figure out.
2. A serial entrepreneur who never gets beyond the startup phase.
3. Someone who boasts about their great business ideas but doesn't follow through with them.

Local business meetups are full of entryprenuers. They hand out business cards with obscure titles like "Chief Rainmaker." If they're still using an aol.com email address, I put them on an even lower rung—"whytryprenuers."

---

no bones (no bonz) *n.*
A job or job offer that's below "bare bones" on the pay scale—somewhere between minimum-wage and zero, or between zero-and minus-whatever. (I.e., you're stuck more out-of-pocket expenses than real revenue.)

After I had gotten laid off, I called a local colleague asking if he could help me at all with my new job search.

Instead of giving me business referrals, he offered me to be a salesperson on-commission for his brand. The catch was, I wasn't going to get paid at all, until he invoiced his clients at the very end. So basically, I would be working for him for months without seeing any pay.

Really? Work for months in someone else's company with no pay and no stake? I need a job where I'm guaranteed a paycheck for my hard work, not a no-bones gig. Good luck, no-bro.

---

nononoshow (no no no show) *v.*
Someone you're scheduled to meet either cancels at the last moment or stands you up several times in a row.

Years ago, I was supposed to meet a director at a marketing organization for potential job opportunities. He kept rescheduling on short notice, with the final time just an hour before we were supposed to meet. When I brought this up with him, his response was, "Gosh, I'm sorry, let's catch up next year."

I passed. Hard. I don't play extended business tag; I won't deal with a nononoshow.

---

overexposured (oh vur x spo shurd) *adj.*
Giving away too much of your time and talent from the promise of fantastic "exposure;" likely, you've deluded yourself into believing this will yield some tremendous opportunities which you'll eventually get paid handsomely for.

I thought my helping out some local non-profits would have gotten me some paid job referrals, but instead, it got me overexposured to more non-profits who also wanted me to do free work for them. Worse, the non-profit where I was a volunteer was paying other businesses, but now they only saw me as someone who would do more free work for them.

---

purrancy (purr en cee) *n.*
The exchange of social capital or sex appeal for real financial gain; or, the belief that attaching yourself to someone with the former will lead to the latter.

Back when I used to work in the search engine marketing industry, I remember the earlier years when companies at conferences would hire models in skimpy tops to walk all around the conference floor, advertising their name. They believed there was purrancy to be gotten from techie marketing attendees, whose own social confidence and sex appeal may have been wanting.

---

rockstar (rock star) *n., adj.*
The term used by a company looking to hire talent well below norm pay rates, pre-stating their fanatical admiration for someone who's easily suckered in by false praise.

Have you seen job announcements like this: "Now hiring rock-stars to manage our clients' social media accounts, shoot video, optimize websites to show up #1 in Google search results, and lift up to 100 pounds—starting at $8.50/hour!"

Seriously, how many ads do you see that use the word "rockstar" in their job descriptions? Job sites need to have a filter word to weed out those jokesters because too many people get sucked in with that shiny word. They become "rockstarstruck."

---

resumess (re zu mess) *n.*
What happens when your resume gets mutilated on the way to a job interview.

I came up with this during a group job interview at my local Apple store. A single mom came in later than the other candidates, apologizing that she didn't have her resume because it got drenched in a rainstorm. I supposed if she had attempted to hand it in as I imagined it, soaked and coming apart in her fingers, it would have been a real resumess.

It hadn't mattered since our interviewers didn't even know that they were supposed to be interviewing us, up until one minute before the actual interview. No one looked at any of our resumes, and the questions they asked sounded as if they were on an LSD trip.

Needless to say, I never got a callback. Apple has always been excellent with customers, but from my experience, they were shitty with job candidates. What a resumess.

---

scambitious (scam beh shuss) *adj.*
Job openings that are listed as "entry level" but demand lots of skillsets and work experience.

How is a position only "entry level" if they require five years of professional work experience even to be considered? That is seriously scambitious.

---

voluntold (vowl un tuld) *n.*
Being pressured by your employer to work for free.

Back when I worked for a retail business, the owner and his acting manager would persistently request the part-time staff "volunteer" for events his business was sponsoring. While he liked to think of it as charity work, he expected the staff to promote business and hock his wares—just not be paid for our time doing it. I semi-politely told the owner that I wouldn't be voluntold what to do.

If you ever come across anyone like that in your job, just do what I did—keep a calm voice and say to them,"I'm sorry, but I'm not a charity and neither are you." They can go volun-tell someone else.

---

tipstortion (tip stor shun) *n.*
When a fast food business pressures you to add a gratuity before any actual food service.

Right after I place my order, Panera Bread forces me into the "guilt-tipping" stage of hitting the NO button instead of a 15%,

20%, or 25% tip for food and service they haven't even provided me with yet. They don't even bus tables there.

Now I think of it more in an extortion sort of way. Like, "It would be a shame for anything to happen to your order." That's just tipstortion. What's next, supermarket checkouts asking for a tip before we get our groceries bagged?

My attitude is, if they expect to get a tip for not actually having done anything yet, they should expect we can eat all of their food without having to first pay for it, either. Maybe we could also request a 20% tip for being such a good customer. (Only fair, right?)

GRANTASMS ARE MOOLAH FOR YOUR MOUTH!

Yay for food!
Grantasms for eats

"Fettuccine Alfredo is macaroni and cheese for adults."

~MITCH HEDBERG (COMEDIAN)

Good culinary experiences make for better conversations and meetups. I like to pay attention to how people consume food—for enjoyment, anticipation, disgust, and remarks. Even lousy food experiences are indeed excellent opportunities for Grantasms—as long as people are sharing your misery, you can crack a funny over it.

"EATING A CROISSANT... Expectation: Fancy and French. Reality: **Crumb apocalypse**."

~INSTAGRAM @WECANNOTEVEN7

While sharing our food experiences is one of the best icebreakers, we're still prone to doing socially awkward things when we're eating and drinking with others. Sometimes it's because what we're consuming fails to live up to our expectations; sometimes it's because we're distracted, and sometimes we've enjoyed ourselves just a bit too much.

I love to create Grantasms for all kinds of food, food combos, situations involving food, foodies fooding with their food, and kung food fighting. A Grantasm can make a bad food experience funny, and a good food experience foogasmic.

Ready to munch? Let's enjoy a Grantasms brunch!

---

bratito (brah tee tow) *n.*
A bratwurst in a tortilla.

I usually make myself a bratito because I've run out of buns, or I fool myself into thinking that 100 fewer calories will make all the difference.

---

brexit (brex it) *v.*
Leaving the house before breakfast.

I'm usually in a sour mood if I've brexit-ed. Unless that is, my boss surprises us with guilt-free snacks at work.

---

crapple (krap ul) *n.*
An apple with a crappy taste, smell, or texture.

Apples are supposed to be crisp on the outside and crunchy-juicy on the inside. We sometimes get a crapple when we purchase a pre-packaged bunch that's woody and undelicious.

frownie (frow nee) *n.*

The face someone makes from eating a gluten-free brownie.

Turn that frownie upside-downie, and plop it into the compost bin!

Truthfully, I like some gluten-free brownies, but my past co-workers make faces when eating them that fall between "sad" and "disgusting."

When I'm on an anti-inflammation diet, frownies helps a little, but you still have to search for ones that aren't loaded with added sweetener. Otherwise, you'll be having another kind of "frownie" when you step on the scale!

---

joe camel (jo cah mul) *n.*

Someone who drinks coffee and smokes at the same time.

If you do this, you are disgusting to me. You are not a misunderstood creative or literary type. You are gross. At the same time —really?

My late dad was a Joe Camel up until my pre-teen years. I would just hate-hate-hate when he would smoke while our family was having breakfast, or when he'd take the family out to McDonald's. (Gawd, I still hate thinking about those aluminum ashtrays.) I couldn't fathom how someone could take a sip of coffee, huff a cigarette, then sip coffee again. I know some people still do it.

Do you want to know what second-hand cigarette smoke smells like after someone has been drinking coffee? Still gross!

Now that we live in North Carolina I don't have as many issues with smokers. Truthfully, I find some tobacco to have a pleasant smell by itself. I have yet to see my first Joe E-Camel—someone who switches between drinking coffee and vaping. That would be "e-gross."

---

lunchoochoo (lun chu chu) *n., v.*
Having to eat your lunch or any other meal, more quickly than usual. (Choo-choo!)

A fellow remote co-worker told me sometimes she only has time to eat lunch quickly during our conference calls. I lunchoochoo sometimes as well, but more like for outside webinars or where they can't see me on webcam.

---

moatmeal (moat meel) *n.*
When your oatmeal looks sunken-in, like the moat formed from whatever liquid you've over-poured into your cereal bowl.

Moatmeal applies to any breakfast cereal. At some point, you're not having breakfast anymore; you're having cold soup with the world's most porous castle.

---

paistrickery (pay strik ur ee) *n.*
When the pastries at fancy bakeries or coffee shops look a lot bigger behind the display window than they do after you've ordered one.

So why do they still have the same amount of calories?? That's like a double-paistrickery.

---

redelicious (ree de lish us) *n.*
When you can take tainted food and make it tasty again.

Redelicious those bruised, middle-aged bananas by making them into banana bread. Mmmm!

My better half loves to "redelicious" food by making soups and stocks out of bruised vegetables. It's a great way to keep the taste and reduce food waste!

soggish (saw gish) *adj.*
The texture of any sandwich you'll get in a boxed lunch at a marketing conference.

One time, I posted on Instagram my soggish sandwich from a marketing conference at the Raleigh, North Carolina, Convention Center. The expo people replied back on Instagram with a personal apology, promising they'd do better. However, they didn't offer me a fresh sandwich for my troubles, nor did they ever say what exactly they'd do differently. So you could say I was not "soggis-fied."

trader jonesing (tray dur joan zing) *adj.*
The anticipation of a new Trader Joe's in your area, or the feeling of withdrawal from being without one.

I love the free samples in the back area of Trader Joe's. I refer to that area in the store as "The Land of the Free, and The Home of the Trade." Even though I've used that line for years, the people behind the counter still laugh, politely, in front of me.

I mostly do trader-jonesing when I'm out of barbecue sauce or red wine. Too bad that the nearest one is now eleven miles away from me, likely making the price savings pale to the extra gasoline. That's what trader-jonesing will do to you.

undelicious (un de lish us) *n.*
When something happens to your once-delicious food that
makes it considerably less so.

*Making food undelicious include: dropping it on the floor,
foreign objects puncturing it, flies crash-landing onto it, or it
sitting out for too long.*

*Here's an idea: maybe restaurants should have different prices
for DELICIOUS, UNDELICIOUS, and REDELICIOUS food?*

---

wafalafel (wah fah lah ful) *n., v.*
Attempting to salvage a meal by scavenging for alternative food
ingredients, with mixed results.

*I discovered that "wafalafels" is an actual food recipe where you
take falafel ingredients and bake them inside a waffle dish.*

*So, let's say you're hungry for waffles, but you only have falafel
mix? Wafalafel it! Problem fixed.*

*What if you like mashed potatoes, but your health regimen
requires you to cut out starches? Wafalafel it! Do like my partner
does for us sometimes and switch it out with cauliflower mash.
(Although, some might consider that as "awful-lafel.")*

---

yum judgment (yum judge mint) *n.*
An anxious decision from eating something pleasurable, while
struggling with moral ramifications or health consequences.

I didn't want to eat at Chick-fil-A because of the surrounding issues for LGBTQ folks. However, being in North Carolina, I kept hearing about how delicious their chicken wrap is. So I decided to try it, once. It was pretty good, alright. I decided that was enough. I don't want my yum judgment to outweigh my sense of social good.

GRANTASMS ARE YOUR WORD COOKIES FOR CHEWY CONVERSATIONS!

OKStupid!
Grantasms for relationshits

OKStupid (oh kay stoo ped) *n.*
A faux pas story, phrase, or word about online dating, mating, and everything in-between or out-tween.

People who know me well, know I was as OKStupid as they come. I was a serial "laywaster."

---

laywaster (lei way stur) n.
Searching for sexual confidence or easy gratification to avoid dealing with essential but uncomfortable things about oneself.

Don't get me wrong, I have had lots of fun and made some real friends to this day, but I got very carried away. So to reign in my bad behavior and fully appreciate what I had, I gave names to my many experiences and observations.

For years I would have conversations with my FWBs. We

shared funny and relatable stories on our "datemating" experiences. I honestly felt there was a need for defining new relationship statuses, shared needs, and not-all-that-uncommon situations.

That is why I'm inspired to share these OKStupid Grantasms—my self-created words that describe the gamut of online dating and hookups, the types of people you'll come across while searching for love and commitment, and new names for how we define relationships in our social era.

GRANTASMS BECAME MY NEW APPROACH TO INTIMATE RELATIONS

I've been in many of the relationship labels you'll find here—the good, bad, and blog-worthy. An original word or phrase helps me enjoy remembering them, or laugh and feel better about an otherwise unenjoyable memory.

I hope you'll enjoy these OKStupid Grantasms as a fun way to navigate modern datemating. You might even discover a fresh way to approach dating and intimacy and pursue your relationship goals.

I think sometimes, we need to feel okay with letting ourselves get a little stupid so we can have wisdom and real relationship smarts, especially for when we find that special someone. Or maybe, a select few. Whatever floats your dinghy.

---

alt-spouses (alt spow sez) *n.*
Two people who have been together a long enough time, but neither are genuinely committed to the relationship.

For 18 months I had an "alt-spouse." She lived with me since her two teenage boys and her ex-husband, her ex-husband's best friend, her ex-husband's friend's wife, and two large sheep-herding dogs all still lived with her.

benefits-with-friendliness (ben eh fits with frend lee nes) *n.*
The situation with a regular or semi-regular sex partner with whom you share a decent social connection.

A "benefits with friendliness" (BWF) is someone you're more likely to have sex with than dinner. A BWF is someone I get along pretty well and have some enjoyable conversations, but we don't yet know each other all that well to put our trust in each other. They're more than a fling and less than a committed friend.

blahtonic (blah than ick) *n.*
A dull "no benefits" relationship.

Sometimes you try to stay friends with someone you formerly had an intimate relationship with, but it just doesn't seem worth maintaining without the sex.

Part of that is also the knowledge that the other person is now having intimate relationships with other people besides you, and you don't have that much else to make up for it. It becomes blahtonic and you eventually part ways, hopefully on amicable terms.

---

boyfind (boy find) *n.*
Not a boyfriend, but has the potential to be one.

I once had a former BWF ask me to give her a name for a relationship that wasn't quite a serious relationship but was holding out for the promise of one.

"He and I like each other a lot, but I feel weird about calling him my 'boyfriend,' maybe it's just too early," she confided in me.

"He's a boyfind," I replied. "You find him boyfriend-worthy so far, but you need to see how things play out before you come on too heavy. Plus, you don't know if he wants the same thing that you do, and it's too early for you to be direct with asking him, right?"

bromenist (bro min ist) *n.*
Someone who's has both progressive feminist and traditional "guy" qualities.

I consider myself a bromenist. I can go to a pro-choice women's empowerment rally, attend a conversation salon while enjoying my craft beer and check a bare knuckle boxing clip on YouTube. I watch HGTV and amuse myself with the sound of my farts, while being courteous enough to excuse myself from the room for the smelly ones; or, know better than to let one rip around mixed company.

I once was told by a politically leftist friend that some feminists aren't keen on hearing "bro" as part of any word, which they associate with frat-house sexism. However, bromenism recognizes and avoids toxic masculinity, without having to treat masculinity as toxic in itself.

I use "bro" as a gender-neutral term, meant to identify behaviors that are traditionally masculine, but not reserved for men, alone. Besides, there's women's MMA now, and I consider them bromenists. (I bet they can fart openly, too.) Feel the bro!

chatterbaiter (chah tur bay tur) *n.*
Someone who gets off messaging people on a dating site, but never follows through on an actual meeting.

The most common kind of chatterbaiter is someone who's secretly in a monogamous relationship and are looking to feel better about themselves without actually "cheating." (Or so, that's how they convince themselves.)

Another kind of chatterbaiter could have severe anxiety or depression issues. Although too apprehensive to actually date, they are really into online chats, where they relish being found desirable but keep an ultra-safe distance from physical contact.

---

cougar math (cu gar math) *n.*
What a middle-aged woman does to figure out if a boy is of a certain age so having sex with him would make her a "cougar."

A female friend told me her cougar math is: half her age + 7. "If he's younger than that and I still have sex with him (or plan to), then I'm a cougar."

---

endorfriend (en dorf rend) *n.*
A friend who gives you an endorphin rush.

I think of my best endorfriends as being the ones that you keep around just because they dare you to do things outside your comfort zone. They may have tons of flaws that make them not ideal to have over for a dinner party. But when you want to either skydive or muffdive, they are your go-to.

friend bunnies (frend buh neez) *n.*
FWBs who have kids of their own.

A "friend bunny" is more fun for me to call a mom-FWB than a "friend-with-benefits." Managing playtime with friend bunnies requires considerably more flexibility and patience, even if you're shacking up together.

girl-get (gurl get) *n.*
A female who makes you feel special, like a girlfriend, but it's too early to call her that.

My book editor asked me, "Why not a 'girlfind?'" I can only speak for the hetero-normative guy perspective when describing females he fancies. That kind of guy would refer to a woman as a "girl-get" because he would feel more of a need to impress his other friends that he's a testosterone-fueled hunter in his date-mating habits, at least while he's still single.

My girl-gets were girl-gones once they found a steady, but I still relished the mutual thrill of the date-mating hunt where no one gets eaten for sport. (Well, I only mean that literally. Or figuratively? Hopefully, you girl-get what I'm saying.)

male snail (mail snayl) *n.*
An old boy-toy.

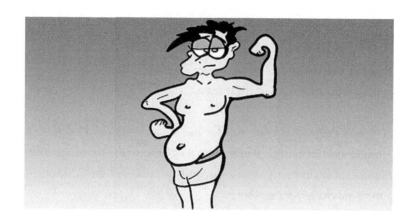

Sometimes a male snail is an FWB who looks considerably younger than his age, and yours.

Or, he can look younger than his age from a distance, but up close you see the visible signs—moobies (man boobs), a spare tire, and hair sprouting in semi-rude places.

Or, it can be that the guy you first found sexy is now lacking something. He could be lazy with his foreplay efforts, can't perform as well as he used to, isn't as well-groomed, and his joints are making clicking noises that interrupt your Netflix shows. You've now entered into a male snail relationship.

I admit I have been that male snail in FWB relationships, the "in-betweener" until a sexier dude comes the woman's way. That's when I feel male-sluggish.

---

neandercall (nee an dur call) *n.*
A text message from a guy who appears on the earlier stage of human evolution. (Also see, "homo-textus-erectus.")

Once at a Meetup.com event for local business folks, I met a

50

woman who was passing through to speak at a corporate function.

"This guy has texted me thirteen times already, and all he says is 'hey,'" she'd bemuse herself. She acted bored with him, but apparently, still found it amusing enough to share his texts to a stranger (me) during happy hour. Otherwise, I guess, she would have just blocked his neandercalls on her phone.

OKCuckold (oh kay cuh cold) *n.*
When the spouse or primary partner of someone posts only the pics of their far-sexier partner on a dating app, to improve their odds at finding someone for threesome or couples fun.

An OKCuckold could already be in an attached relationship, and their partner may be oblivious to what's happening. However, the OKCuckold doesn't consider that to be cheating; because to them, it's just an impersonal fantasy, until shit gets real.

OKCuckit, already.

---

significant better (cig nif eh cant beh tur) *n.*
A significant other you hold in higher esteem than yourself.

My own significant better is financially savvy, highly ethical, great social company (some of the time), and a fantastic cook. That's significantly better-ish if you ask me!

---

sour dough (sowur dow) *n.*

An older man or woman who paid someone to be their trophy girlfriend or their boy-toy, and is now pissed because the arrangement is over.

I remember meeting a "sour dough"—a financially independent divorced woman—at a local chamber of commerce mixer. She would gush on and on about how her early-twenty-something boy-toy had so much more stamina in bed, and was so much better looking than her ex-husband. When the short-lived relationship was over, she would then complain about how immature he was, along with many other previously unmentioned faults.

---

spousish (spow sish) *n.*

How you refer to your partner when you've been together long enough that it's just silly to refer to each other as boyfriend/girlfriend, even though you both choose not to be married.

My partner, Karen, and I are spousish. We both still tell each other "I love you" and "fuck off" on the same day. If you crave a label with a little more distinction and tradition, you can also refer to your male partner as "hubbish." (That's hubbish, not rubbish.)

vanillish (vah nil ish) *n.*

Someone who's mostly into "vanilla" sex but occasionally enjoys some variety; or, is open to trying new things with the right partner.

If you fall more into extra-vanillish sexual activities, that's called "vanilla with nuts." Extra-extra-vanillish is "vanilla with nuts and extra toppings." Blahnilla is one position and that's it.

How do I know these things, you ask? Church? Goat yoga? Scream therapy?

GRANTASMS MAKE IT A-OK TO BE STUPID WITH SOCIAL SMARTS!

ADHDelirious!
Grantasms for distractions

My thoughts have thoughts. I just wish sometimes they'd tell me what they're thinking.

WHAT'S FUNNY ABOUT ADHD?

- It's a birthday present with trip-wires all over the gift-wrapping.
- It's a cool uniform given to you by aliens from outer space, containing super powers waiting to be unlocked, but you lost the instruction manual.
- It's a camera with the focus broken, yet catches super-intriguing shots.

- Sometimes it's a fun roller coaster ride; other times it's an exasperating mountain climb.
- It can make you feel hopeful and hopeless at the same time.
- Oh yeah, I hear squirrels are now tired of being associated with it.

THE NAME IS THE THING

How we name things shapes our perspective. That's why I like to come up with special words for my own ADHD that make me laugh and learn— both from my mistakes and achievements.

Overthinkitis, interruptus rex, ooh-look-so-shiny-syndrome, brain-on-bongo-drums, squirrel-on-crack, instant-gratification-monkey-on-my-back, and Attention-Dynamic-Hyperfocused-Dude.

I don't lose stuff... stuff loses itself.

Twisted words have proven to be the most successful way for me to manage my ADHD. They transform something depressing into being creative and funny, and so much easier to face head-on. I am empowered by it.

That's why I have these words, to be more playfully mindful of my condition so I can be more intentional with my actions. It works for so many adults who feel overwhelmed with distractions, and could use a kind, creative, helping hand.

Whether you have ADHD or behaviors akin to it from traversing our ADHD-like world, if you have good intentions and wandering *a-tension*, I hope these ADHDelirous Grantasms can make you laugh and relate to what we're all dealing with—and possibly re-wire your brain for the better, as I continue to do so with mine.

Welcome to my ADHD world—let's play!

---

adhdeesus freak (ay dee h dee zus freek) *n.*
A person who talks too much about having ADHD.

I'm so guilty of this. Like a religious zealot who feels compelled to bring up Jesus in every conversation, an adhdeesus freak will bring up their ADHD, unprompted and repeatedly. They could use an adhdeetox.

Take for example, job interviews. Too early and often, I would impulsively mention my condition.

Interviewee: Thank you Mr. Crowell for your application. So tell me, about your interest in this posi—

Me: I HAVE ADHD!

Okay, that's an exaggeration, but you know what I mean. It can be as annoying as someone substituting the word ADHD in any conversation with "Jesus" or "bananas."

---

appnesia (app nee shuh) *n.*

1. Downloading an app, only to be flabbergasted later as to what prompted you to do so.
2. Having so many apps on your phone that you forget why you put them there.
3. When an app notification makes you forget what you were supposed to be doing.

Why the hell did I ever think I needed the app for "Places I've Pooped?" (Yes, there's an app for that.) Seriously, look at all the apps on your phone right now. Can you honestly remember what they all do? When your appnesia is so common that it's more the rule than the exception, it's time to get an appendectomy.

---

carjackass (kar jak ass) *n.*
When you open up a car in a parking lot and sit down in the seat, only to realize that you just opened up someone else's car.

Walking to the car from the movie, the car next to me beeped, and I just opened the unlocked door and sat down in the passenger seat, thinking my own partner had just pressed door unlock button to our car. Nothing awkward about the couple staring at you because you are actually in their car, or your partner being confused about why you got into a stranger's car as she points to our car in the next aisle.

Yes, I have done this. I've also had some carjackass open my passenger car door while I'm still in the driver's seat.

---

funcrastination (fun cra te nay shun) *n.*
When you keep putting off finishing your old project or to-do item because the new one is shinier.

ADHD folks like myself are huge funcrastinators. Sometimes we put off doing something because we're nervous about it. Other times, we are so attracted to what's new and right in front of us that it's "shininess" takes our attention off of what we may already be enjoying doing. I funcrastinated with writing this very book for years, because everything newer I'd see would appear shinier to me.

---

gymnesia (jim nee zhuah) *n.*

Opening up every unlocked locker in you local fitness center because you forgot which locker you placed your exercise bag in.

I would always do this when I forgot to bring a combination padlock in my gym bag. I used to suffer from gymnesia so much that I must make other gym members in the locker room suspect I'm either a thief or a crazy person. I did eventually learn to give myself a few seconds to focus closely on my locker number, so I suffer from gymnesia way less now.

---

imboretant (em boar tant) *adj.*

Boring but important.

Filing taxes is imboretant, so I now leave all the financial stuff for my significant other to figure out.

---

indirections (en dur ek shuns) *n.*

When your GPS sends you far off course from your intended destination.

Why does Google Maps seem like its default is to show me same-name locations hundreds of miles from the local store I'm trying to navigate to? Is it trying to give me an indirections option because it thinks I'm bored and need to take a road trip, or maybe it's because that closer store doesn't want me there?

(My partner also wants to add another definition. "Indirections: when Google tells you to turn into a subdivision just to go around the roundabout, then have you come right back out, and continue driving on the same road in the same direction you were just in.")

---

maybeD (may bee dee) *n.*
A person who talks about ADHD like it's a passing thing.

"Oh, yeah, I get ADHD sometimes," says the MaybeD. "Just the other day I misplaced my car keys."

Some MaybeDs simply don't know any better and are open to learning, versus the MaybeDicks who aren't.

---

messytasking (mess ee tas keen) *v.*
Multitasking with less-than-favorable results. (i.e., being sloppy with your multi-tasking.)

I used to be a horrible messytasker. I've typed and spilled coffee all over my laptop keyboard while watching a webinar and doing instant messaging, and probably three other things that I'm not going to admit here. I now believe that anyone who says they are a successful multi-tasker—like an ex-boss of mine—is really a messytasker in denial. They just have other people who are responsible for cleaning up their messes.

notifriction (no teh frik shun) *n.*
The anxiety felt from too many notifications coming out of
your digital devices.

*I think we all are searching for the balance of being alerted to
things that are important at the right time, versus "Oh, that's
cool," or "Hey, you might want to buy this," or "Someone on a
dating app just winked at you."*

*A lot of notifriction is preventable when it's coming from our
digital devices. It's harder to deal with bosses and coworkers who
expect you to be always-on, immediately responding to an IM or
email, or any comment on a social media channel. Back then my
notifriction was compounded by foolish people who expected me
to instantaneously react to all of their pings and buzzes and pop-
ups, like some kind of digitally-enslaved Pavlov's dog.*

*There goes my phone right now. Breathe, Grant. Don't recognize
the number? Likely, it's a robocall. Put my phone notifications
back on "Do not disturb," except for the important folks who are
worth being notifriction'd by.*

---

stupid power (stew ped pow ur) *n.*
The extraordinary power of ADHD people and creative
people, in general, to take risks where others succumb to social
anxiety.

*I remember one time when I was called "stupid" by a supervisor
at a part-time college job I had. Not because my on-the-job
conduct, mind you. I had a political cartoon published in the*

University newspaper, and she was fearful that some politically-minded people in one of the other departments would be angry by it. She threatened to get me fired, to which I reminded her we were on a University campus, and free speech was a protected right. (Fortunately it eventually blew over; I left a year later on good terms between us.)

I've been called stupid many times in my life by people who's main reasoning was, "But what will others think?"

True creativity has to come with a willingness to share your stupid power—be weird, be vulnerable. Don't be deterred by someone who might call you stupid because they're too afraid to risk anything themselves. Just be aware of the potential consequences and how to deal with them, otherwise that would make you stupid-powerless.

synapstuck (sin napp stuhk) *n.*
When the synapses in your brain don't function correctly, which for an ADHD person is 90-99% of the time.

At an old retail job, I found myself struggling with punching in the code on the break room door at work. My then-boss came by and did it for me. I then remembered the code and felt silly. My boss empathized with me since he also has ADHD and has done the same thing. "It's just those synapses not working right," he said. Yes, he was correct; I was synapstuck.

---

whiteout (why tout) *n.*
Blanking out while seemingly conscious. You forget what you're doing while in the middle of doing it.

Early in my relationship with my partner (and before I was getting back on medication and counseling for my ADHD), I remember when we were all packed in the car and about to embark on a long road trip.

"Dear," she asked me, "will you go back in the house and make sure all the lights are turned off?"

I went upstairs to check on the lights, and then I got distracted. I checked my email since my computer was still on. Then I saw my unfolded laundry since it was still on the bed. Then I got a text message and was answering it in the bedroom. I completely forgot that she was still waiting in the car, and I blanked out that we were supposed to be driving out to her parents' house. It was like some mischievous whiteout force had erased my memory.

Now whenever I forget what I'm doing, I jokingly say I'm having a whiteout. I don't beat myself up anymore. I laugh about it, and guess what—I remember it better next time. I actually become motivated to fix the problem behavior the next time I see it coming.

GRANTASMS KEEP THE ADHD AT BAY!

Digital douches!
Grantasms for interwebz

digital douche (dih gih tul doosh) *n.*

1. An online faux pas from either human or computer error, or a combination of both.
2. An internet asshole.

Digital douches fall into two categories: those who don't know any better, and those who don't care.

Despite all my years working in digital communications, I sometimes struggle to recognize social cues, especially online. Sometimes my emotions get the better of me, causing me to post something in haste and poor judgment. I wish I could take it back, or that I had an internal pause button.

GOOD INTENTIONS, WANDERING E-TENSION

Many of us go online with the best plans, but we find ourselves making faux pas. Sometimes we're just not tech-savvy enough, or socially stylish enough, about navigating our digital ecosystem.

NETIQUIT?

Netiquette—how well we carry ourselves online that is considered by us and our peers as socially acceptable—is crucial for healthy communication. The problem is that netiquette is too easy to forget—not just because we don't have to deal with discomfort of face-to-face reactions, but also because it's very difficult to agree on what's actually socially acceptable behavior online.

"Everybody online lives somewhere."

~CHRIS TOLLES, CO-FOUNDER OF TOPIX

THE CONSEQUENCES OF SOCIAL SLOBBERY

While social media has made information and people online way more accessible, it's also made us far less *assessable* of our behavior. It's too easy to take each other way too much for granted; we don't pause enough to reflect on how our actions online might affect others, or how frequently spending time online affects our socio-emotional health.

I would be hypocritical to make this a diatribe against social media. After all, I used to work in it. My ego was fed by it, and still is to some degree. I've had so much instant gratification from it and have also made some long-term friendships out of it, and I've also broken up some friendships over it. Social media is an I-like-you-and-fuck-you relationship.

SOMETHING GOOD FROM EFF-ING UP

Good experiences with social media can bring empathetic people together to share a laugh and give insights into more constructive ways to deal with assholes. Occasionally we might have an epiphany and realize that the asshole we're railing against may be us.

These "digital douche" Grantasms are labels I create to laugh about the honest faux pas, the tech failures, and the crappy side of our digital society. When I share a "digital douche" Grantasm, I feel less stressed, empowered, and relieved. They make me more mindful and intentional of how I approach my day—online and offline.

I hope these Grantasms will make you laugh out loud and discover some new ideas (and many words) of your own about how to approach "playful mindfulness" for our ever-over-expanding digital culture. You might even catch a digital douche and transform it into a creative delight—a word invention all of your own.

Let's Faux-play!

---

dissconnected (diss con nek ted) n.

1. The feeling of being dissed—i.e., exploited by someone—after you've accepted their connection request and given them access to your personal life, online.
2. Disconnecting from someone on a social media network due to feelings of mistreatment or neglect.
3. Feeling misunderstood through the limitations of technology, social media, and human emotional intelligence.

I wish I had an option to require people who want to connect to me on a one-to-one basis to write something original that shows they actually looked at my profile. If I could see that they hadn't bothered to do that, I would like to have a "dissconnect" button that would also let them know why I've done so. Someone might rack up so many dissconnects that they would have to take a mandatory netiquette class to be allowed back into the social network; otherwise, they could only be allowed to use it on a limited basis. (Maybe like an observe-only, look-don't-touch restricted mode.)

---

distwaction (dis twack shun) n.

1. Distracted by social media
2. A tweet meant to distract people from serious stuff.

While the mainstream media gets distwacted by the President's rambling tweets, an executive order goes out that has far more impact on people's lives.

An occassional distwaction for me is when I'm at a conference trying to learn, and the hosts are encouraging people to tweet or Instagram during the actual event, while a speaking session is going on.

---

fitbitching (fit bitch) v.

What you do when your fitness activity tracking device doesn't work correctly, and you only find out after you're done with your workout.

I'll sometimes hear my partner fitbitching when she wears her Fitbit, and it didn't record her last three miles because her battery died. She got me to get my own fitbit, but I don't gripe nearly as much as she does if I forget to set it up before a workout. I might get a little fitbummed, but that's about it.

---

instagramification (en sta gram if eh cay shun) n.

Someone who is so pleased with themselves over their Instagram pics that they come across as being really stuck-up or annoying.

When someone gets in front of you at a big event and blocks your view, while taking multiple selfies making kissy-lips and typing two dozen vanity hashtags—like #ontopoftheworld, #whowantstobeme, and #kimkardashiandouble—that's when their instagramification should be treated as a misdemeanor offense. (Or, at least, one free whack to the head from everyone whose view they blocked. "We were trying to watch something big going down, but the gal's instagramification ruined it for us.")

---

internot (en tur not) n.
When your internet stops working.

I used to work for a do-it-yourself book publishing platform, where it was commonplace for our internet to crash on us. One day I just shouted, "It's not an internet, it's an interNOT!"

---

meanameme (mean' a meam) n.
An extra-mean picture that goes viral.

The majority of memes are done to playfully ridicule human behavior. Some meanamemes I've seen are so nasty and devoid of boundaries that they make the sender look ridiculous, sometimes garnering sympathy for their intended target of derision.

---

napp (nah puh puh) n.
Taking a rest break free of all digital devices.

Once in a chatroom for a company I worked for remotely, someone asked our workgroup if there was an app that would tell you when you need more sleep. I typed, "Yeah, it's called a napp." (*Some people in our group actually asked me where they could find it online since it wasn't showing up in their search results.*) *You could say a person who takes regular restbreaks from their digital devices is a nappster.*

---

nonference (non fur ence) n.

- A conference call where you're the only who bothered to show up (or the others can't get off mute).
- An event where you're the only one who speaks out.

When I failed to realize that I had placed everyone on mute, I had a nonference entirely of my own doing. Hello? Helllllooooo? Uh-oh.

If I'm leading a web conference and I can't get anyone to talk during the Q&A portion, I'll consider that a nonference as well.

---

oddcast (odd cast) n.
A podcast you listen to and wonder what the hell you just heard.

One time, I listened to a popular marketing oddcast where the guest said "y'know" over 300 times in 28 minutes! It drove me so crazy that I went back and marked every instance, and then wrote a lengthy article about the experience on my Medium.com blog.

---

polyappory (paw lee app or ree) n.
Being in love with multiple apps at the same time on your phone (and trying to make them all get along).

I'm used to be into polyappory. I would wish my LinkedIn Jobs app could work with my Glassdoor reviews app so I could save myself some time going back-and-forth between them.

This can also apply to having multiple dating-hookup apps and you try to keep track of all your profiles and conversations between them.

---

schizofriendia (skit zo frend ee uh) n.

1. Going crazy trying to get friends and followers on your social media accounts.
2. "Friending" or following yourself in another Facebook account you already own.
3. Opening up a dummy Facebook account to give yourself faux accolades.

Even I, a former social media professional, have had a temporary bout of schizofriendia. One time I had accidentally used a dummy business profile to "Like" my personal profile on Facebook.

What really annoys me with schizofriendia is the intentional stuff. Many unscrupulous entrepreneurs today send "friend" or "connection" requests to tons of people they meet at networking events, mainly so they can spam them instead of building genuine relationships. Maybe that's more of sociopathic-friendia?

---

social beef (so' shul beef) n.
Picking a fight about something or someone on a social media platform. Or, merely venting frustration with social media and networking.

Growing up in Hawai'i, I remember the pidgin-English phrase for challenging someone to a physical fight was, "Like beef?!" On social media, we substitute keyboards for in-person verbal spats or fisticuffs.

I once produced a mini YouTube series called, "What's Your Social Beef?" In it, I got five random strangers at a coffee shop to share their most frustrating personal issues about social media on camera. You can still find that series on my YouTube channel and watch us all social beefing.

---

text message (text miss edge) n.

1. A text message sent to the wrong person.
2. A text message that was missed, misinterpreted or misunderstood.

I had a friend text message me an angry rant by mistake; my name was similar to the person for whom she intended it.

I've done that myself many times. Many years ago, I had two Facebook chats going on—one with a coaching group, and one with a casual friend. I was talking with the casual friend about adult-y stuff involving sex, but I sent it to the coaching group by mistake.

---

tweety-bird (twee' tee bird) n., v.
A tweet where someone gets flipped off.

I have tweety-birded people on Twitter, especially companies who steal my published articles and try to pass themselves off as the original authors.

(Yeah, that word is commonly known an animated fictional yellow canary in the Warner Bros. Looney Tunes and Merrie Melodies series of animated cartoons. However, I gave it a new definition with my own personal story, so it's STILL A GRANTASM!)

twezident (twez ee dent) n.
A president who is addicted to posting on Twitter.

We should just refer to our twezident as "Twonald Twump, the Twumander in Tweef." (I've heard some virulent anti-Trumpers refer to him as "Orange Twitler." I could go for "Twezident Twizzle-Dizzle.")

---

websore (web soar) n.
An ugly looking website, or a site that is a pain-in-the-arse to navigate.

Any website that doesn't fit on a phone's web browser automatically qualifies as a websore. (Yes, sadly, they still exist.)

I worked for a company that was such a websore that I couldn't send it any traffic from our social media channels; it would surely have killed the leads. I imagined the front page having an apology in big bold letters saying, "We're very websore-y for your crappy experience here. But there's good news! You can look forward to a brand-new website, someday. We're still in our third year of beta testing it, but our boss keeps talking about how it's coming out... (Help us, please—we need to find better jobs.)"

GRANTASMS ARE YOUR TE-TOX FOR DIGITAL DOUCHERY!

Super socialize me!
Grantasms for gerks

gerk (gerk)

n. A person who identifies as a *geek, nerd, and dork* whom is striving to be a remarkable social citizen.

v. To get all geeky, nerdy, and dorky with someone with whom you are looking to create a social bond.

I am proud to call myself a gerk. Here's how I gerk it to people:

- A "geek" is your passion
- A "nerd" is your expertise
- A "dork" is yourself (i.e., you being you).

Learning to be mindful of social context—i.e., knowing when to be yourself and when to blend in, accepting feelings of awkwardness, and bringing empathy to your actions, is the path to becoming a fine gerk.

I especially hope you'll enjoy these particular Grantasms. They come from my own attempts to be more mindful and intentional with my communications, while staying my gerky self.

Online or offline, it's all real as long as we're really trying. (And sometimes, not trying *too* hard).

---

automagic (ah tow ma jic) *adj.*
What successful people seem to do effortlessly.

Automagic people know how to "think like a prep cook"
regarding all the repetitive things in their work. Instead of
labeling someone a "productivity specialist," it would be cooler
to call such a person an "automagician," don'tcha think?

---

begotchas (bee got chas) *n.*
People listing themselves as beginners in a Meetup group when
they are actually more advanced than they let on.

I've been around different kinds of begotchas in several groups
on Meetup.com. Sometimes the begotchas join groups thinking
they'll find someone attractive who will be impressed by them,
and they'll think to themselves, "easy date." Other begotchas are
people who got kicked out of the group, because they never
worked on their social skills so that they'd actually learn how to
fit in.

facetag (fays tag) *v.*
A nametag you draw a cartoon face of yourself.

Whenever I'm at a party or networking, I am always asking for a blank nametag so I can create my own facetag. I am the one reaching for the marker pen to draw a cartoon of the exaggerated, but still genuine, "me."

When my partner and I were invited to attend a cooking Meetup where the theme was French food, I drew a cartoon of myself on the name tag with a snooty mustache and an oversized beret. It didn't exactly look like me, but it had my personality and was appropriate humor for the event theme.

People say that they never forget a face, and I'd like to believe that includes a sketch of a cartoon face. I have the creative advantage of being a cartoonist in college, and I still enjoy cartooning as a hobby. I can draw a cartoon face of myself with any marker pen on any sticky label.

Now whenever I'm at parties, people tell me that they remember me by my facetag. Or, they'll ask me, "Where's your facetag?"

An old-high school friend told me he thinks my facetags are like selfies—before there were phone cameras!

---

fox with friends (ee vil beel zee bub) *v.*
The game you play when you watch a political news show and see who's first to shout at the screen.

Yes, this is an actual game. I play "fox with friends" with my partner. We can even do it with the sound off and just go by the headlines running across the bottom.

---

immoral support (e mor all suh port) *n.*
Someone who encourages you to misbehave.

I remember the guy who shot himself in the head with a nail gun so he could get his Facebook Live to go viral. The news story mentioned the immoral support of his girlfriend and Facebook fans to do the fatal deed.

R-O-Y (arr oh why) *n.*
Return on you.

ROY *derives from the standard business acronym, ROI—"return on investment." ROY isn't calculated as a financial metric. Instead, it speaks to defining and connecting our personal values to our goals, which are evaluated by daily self-reflection. It's about what really matters to you.*

I especially value my own ROY for how I measure personal growth with professional success. I set my ROY goal with writing and publishing this book.

---

shitpathy (shit pah thee) *n.*
A sanctimonious attempt at sympathy.

Shitpathy is when someone goes up to a homeless person begging for spare change and says, "Just pray to God, he'll take care of you." Or when a politician auto-tweets out "our thoughts and prayers" immediately after yet another school shooting.

---

social style (so shul sty ul) *n.*
A distinctive approach to developing one's own style for social relationships, helping you navigate between organic and digital life.

Social style marries tech savvy with social thinking and positive interaction with other people. It's an ideal character trait to reach beyond the screen and remember you're communicating with another human being.

---

social word chef (so shul wurd shef) *n.*
Someone who has a way with words that others find delicious.

I have food on the brain a lot, which is likely why I aspire to be regarded as a social word chef. It's also why I think of all my word creations as thought-for-food.

---

solidude (saul i dood) *n.*
Someone who appears as a calm and collected individual because they're comfortable with being by themselves, in solitude.

One of my business coaches, Bryan Kramer, explained the difference between solitude and loneliness. "Solitude has a big part to play in a healthy lifestyle; if we can learn to be at ease with ourselves in solitude then we can reap the benefits of 'turning off' and unwinding." I know he's one cool solidude.

GRANTASM STRONG AND GERK ON!

Farty party!
Grantasms for poof

"Can you think of a single situation, no matter how grave, where the atmosphere would not be instantly shattered with a loud fart—or a drawing of a butt? There is no faster way to create universal common ground."

~EUNY HONG, AMERICAN JOURNALIST

Everybody farts. Can you remember the last time you did?

Sometimes we fart accidentally; we can't always help it. Once a fart comes out, you can't put a fart back in. Why not laugh about it?

I AM A PROUD FARTIST

My partner and I casually fart in each other's presence. When both of us fart, we say we're having a farty party. We make a game of naming our farts or classifying the farts of others.

"If you can fart in front of somebody, you know that they love you."

~THUNDERCAT, AMERICAN MUSICIAN

We also make up wild stories about the kind of farty parties we'd host and the people we'd invite. Maybe one day we'll write a kids' book of fart poems. Here's one of ours.

Mr. Farty's Party
I can sing, and I can run
I can make sounds from my bum
I can fart as loud as Dad
I can fart it makes me glad.

I would have watched more *Sesame Street* if they'd done some fart songs. As adults, we know there's always the time when someone inadvertently farts in mixed company. Why not turn it into an icebreaker? (Or, a "windbreaker?")

These Farty Party Grantasms are my creative inspiration for turning smells into smiles; you can aim to please while cracking a breeze. Take a whiff, enjoy a blast and don't get too gassed!

---

artisan cheese cutter (ar ti zan cheez cu tur) *n.*
A hi-falootin' name for a smelly farter, or someone who eats a gourmet meal before they pass gas.

Calling myself an artisan cheese cutter is my way of making farts during a fine-dining experience just a little less awkward. Or maybe, more awkward? Either way, I'm amused. I've been tempted to say to guests that our dining experience comes with an artisan cheese cutter, depending on how the evening goes.

---

farticus (far ti cuss) *n.*
A jacked-up, hardcore fitness buff who farts while exercising or playing contact sports.

There's a 50-50 chance I will become a farticus when I'm doing squats, doesn't matter what I've eaten beforehand.

---

fartiquette (far ti kit) *n.*
Being considerate of others when you're farting.

Apologizing that you are about to let one rip, or just did, and then rolling down the car windows, is a minimum level of farti-

quette. Bragging that you let out a mean fart, isn't. (See "gasshole.")

---

foggy style (fawh gee sti ul) *adj.*
Farting during sex.

Come on, I know I'm not the only one who's had foggy style sex. It can also happen when going down on your partner, aka "queefing." Anytime one of you has your legs spread far and wide; you're just sucking in air that's going to come out eventually.

---

gasshole (gas hol) *n.*
Someone who's very inconsiderate with their farting.

A gasshole is the guy who goes on a long road trip with people and eats foods he knows will make his farts smell. (I obviously have no personal experience with that, and don't believe my partner if she says otherwise.)

---

love stinks (luv stinkz) *n.*
Farts that happen while making out.

Love stinks are usually forgivable if you're in the act of having sex and are either close to finishing or making your partner orgasmic, so you don't have to excuse yourself from the bed. Love stinks that happen before or after sex, however, do require getting your ass out of bed and turning on the fan.

---

smarty farty pants (smar tee far tee pantz) *n.*
Someone who comes up with a credible explanation for what that strange smell or noise was that they swear didn't come from them.

I confess I've sometimes been too embarrassed to admit when I accidentally farted, especially those silent and deadly ones. Rather than leaving the area as I should, I would act like I smelled something strange before anyone else did, then I look around to see what's the most likely scapegoat. It could be a domesticated animal, a human baby, an ornery grampa, or a person too far away from us to matter.

Admittedly, I'm often not successful when I attempt this, making me less of a smarty fartypants and just a smelly dumb-ass.

---

smell talk (smel tawk) *n.*
Having a conversation when farting ensues.

I remember interviewing Microsoft rep at a video marketing conference. I had terrible gas that day. The camera had captured a close-up of his painful look while he was in mid-sentence. The smell-talk was priceless.

---

vahoohoo (vah hoo hoo) *n., v.*

1. *n.* A vaginal fart, (a.k.a., queefing).
2. *v.* To fart out of one's vahoohoo lips (a.k.a., the vagina).

A lower, softer noise characterizes "queefs." A vahoohoo is louder and prouder.

TEN MORE GRANTASM FART NAMES

Because why the fart not?

1. Breakfast in Bed (morning farts)
2. Creaky Old Door (slowly letting one out)
3. The Al Capone (semi-automatic gun)
4. Powder Puff (a girl trying hard to hold it in)
5. The Assassin (extreme hang time)
6. Dirty Larry (a "shart")
7. Marching Band (multiple farts that sound like tubas during band practice)
8. McSteamy Café (a type of fart that sounds drippy and lets steam out, or you swear it did.)
9. The Heinz (like squeezing a ketchup bottle)
10. His Fault (when a woman farts)

GO GRANTASM SOME WORD SMELLS OF YOUR OWN!

Oops poops!
Grantasms for #2

Yes, after writing a chapter about something inspirational and profound as farting, I turn to poop. Poop is a silly word for something we all have to do, or we'd explode and die.

However, I wasn't going to call this chapter "Poop, or Explode and Die!" That would be a turn-off. Even more of a turn-off would be having your obituary say you left poop everywhere.

Where was I? Oh, yeah...

EVERYBODY POOPS

We're all poop machines. We poop in all different shapes, sizes, smells, and colors (sometimes in a single poop).

Sometimes our poop is like a Cold Stone Creamery store, and it comes with toppings—from what we ate the night before, or even days back. Poop is what we once were, and will be again, and again, and again. Poop is us even when it's out of us. Even if you just pooped, there's probably still some left in you right now.

"You are all made of real poop."

~ANNE FRANK

See? If Anne Frank can joke and be profound about poop while hiding from Nazis, you certainly don't have an excuse not to!

POOP TRAVELS

I remember traveling through Europe with Karen and seeing the paid restroom facilities everywhere, with attendants and turnstiles. It makes me fascinated with our own cultural approach to poop.

As a runner/jogger, this has been an actual need for me. I wonder if people here in America could be allowed to make money if they'd let others poop in their business establishment, or even their own house. Why not? When ya gotta go, right?

Instead of Airbnb, you could have "AirbnP?"

What if you need someone to drive you to an open bathroom stall? Instead of Uber, you could have "Poober?"

I may have lost some of my readers here. Regardless...

I'M PROUD OF MY POOPS

Well, some of them. I'm blessed to be in a happy and healthy committed relationship where we can play with each other's poop. (By "play" I mean we laugh and joke about it.) For us coming up with new poop names is a fun game, and we have no shortage of smelly stuff for inspiration.

Here's me dumping some oopsie poopsie Grantasms on you, stink-free (hopefully!)

---

alphashit (al fah shit) *v.*, *n.*
Spelling out letters of the alphabet with your poop.

A certain someone I know once boasted of being able to spell out the letter P and Q while on the toilet. (Talk about minding your P's and Q's, right?) I told her that it's my goal to alphashit all 26 letters. Then, I'll move onto upper-case, and then I'll move on to numbers and syntax.

---

buttstorm (butt storm) *n.*
Having a creative inspiration while fighting the bodily urge for defecation.

Okay, who seriously admits to this stuff, other than a guy writing a word book? I will say the combination of having diarrhea with a client deadline counts as a buttstorm.

---

cheesy doodie (chée zee doo dee) *n.*
A poop that comes out while farting.

I also refer to this as a "downtown orange-brown," but that doesn't sound as cute and cuddly as saying cheesy doodie.

grey poupon (grey poo pawn) *n., v.*

1. An old man sitting on a toilet, or feeling like one because it's taking a long time.
2. Pooping out something you really shouldn't have eaten.

Pardon me, did you just "grey poupon?"

---

multicrapping (mul tee crap een) *v.*

1. Feeling the need to do something else while in the act of pooping.
2. When you poop, then get up, realize you need to poop more, get up, and realize you need to poop yet again.

Sometimes when running through forest trails, the constant jarring of my butt makes me need find a semi-secluded spot where I can #2 it. However, I usually still had whatever podcast I'm listening to blaring in my ears. I thought to myself, there isn't any need for me to be multicrapping out in the woods when someone could be coming by at any moment. Plus, I have one less hand free to wipe with whatever leaves I can grab.

Other days, my bum takes me on a downhill ski slope to crazy-town. Having to excuse myself for the 3rd time because I'm multi-crapping makes some people roll their eyes about what I must have eaten.

paloop (pah loop) *n., v.*

1. A really slow poop.
2. A poop that only comes out in bits at a time.
3. A dad, grandad, or uncle that takes a long time to poop (and hogs the bathroom.)

I paloop whenever I'm stuck on the toilet for several minutes or more, waiting for the damn thing to come all the way out.

---

pooetry slam (pu eh tree slam) *n.*
Throwing in a mention of poop at a poetry slam event.

Take, for example, this time I poetry-crashed an event with this poop poem:

> I can sing, I can run
> I make brownies from my bum
> I can poop as big as Dad
> I can poop it makes me glad.

If you can throw in a mention of poop in a haiku, you got yourself a "pooku." Take this other one I did, called, "Dog Owners Beware!" It was inspired by when we lived in a townhome residence. Some of our neighbors would let their dogs shit on our lawns without cleaning it up themselves, even though we had designated doggie-bin spots all around us. (Talk about shitty neighbors, right?)

Bag it, tag it, throw
it in the bin. You don't? Be
ware! We'll do you in.

---

poop coin (poop koin) *n.*
A Euro coin used for a pay toilet.

*I learned on my trip to Europe that if you don't have some poop
coins handy for when you absolutely gotta go, you have to take
poop cover somewhere.*

*I really liked having poop coins. Wouldn't it be cool if we could
all buy poop coins here in the U.S.A., where we could use them
whenever we wanted to go into any establishment whose
restrooms would be posted: "Reserved for paying customers?"
Maybe for a few poop coins, we could get a premium poop stall
with sealed door and walls, soft toilet paper, and Wi-Fi?*

---

poop tweet (poop tweet) *n.*
A tweet sent out at 3 a.m. or other strange hour—a thought that
probably should have been slept on, but you felt that you just
had to get it out.

Presidents aren't the only ones doing poop tweets. I think that any tweet between the hours of 2–4 a.m. in someone's time zone should automatically be filtered and branded with a poop emoji. (I like saying "poopjamoji.")

---

poopsy daisy (poop cee day zee) *n.*
What you exclaim when a poop doesn't flush the whole way down.

"Poopsy daisy!" That's fun to say when someone opens the toilet after you've used it and complains about your leftover crap. Now, I don't recommend that you poopsy-daisy in a host's guest bathroom, or worse, in their master bathroom—not if you want to leave a good impression.

---

poopygamist (poop pee gah mist) *n.*
Someone who uses two or more toilets in a house or small office.

Our townhome has three toilets—one downstairs and two

upstairs (in the master and guest bathrooms). While it would make sense to use only one upstairs for easier cleaning duties, I'd rather be a poopygamist and enjoy the convenience of wherever's closest.

---

poop surprise (poop sir pri z) *n.*
When you open the toilet cover and are greeted by an un-flushed poop.

My partner and I still get into arguments about who was responsible for our poop surprise. I'm starting to think it may be a shitty ghost.

---

shitpathy (shit pah thee) *n.*
Feeling sympathetic for someone because they're constipated.

Some of our foster cats get constipated a lot. I felt such shitpathy when our furry felines are struggling to take a dump. It sucks to be literally "full of shit."

(Say, did you notice this word appeared in an earlier chapter? Goes to show that Grantasms are versatile—they can have more than one definition. Or, defecation-ition! YEAH YEAH, GROAN GROAN GROAN YOUR POOP BOAT.)

---

shittytasking (shéh tee taz keen) *n.*
Working through the urge to hit the restroom.

I remember many years ago I was a featured speaker at a search engine marketing conference. I badly needed to use the bathroom, but it was time for me to present. I want to say I did some impressive shittytasking while I shifted my dress pants side to side while speaking, but the audience may have noticed my severe discomfort.

---

sloopy (sléw pee) *n.*
A poop that runs slowly down the side of the bowl and you have trouble flushing throughly.

A sloopy is usually the result of a soft poop that won't shoot straight down. This kind of sloopy is not to be confused with the 1965 music lyrics by the McCoys for "Hang On Sloopy." Although when you read those lyrics, they do seem rather fitting for a sloopy shitting.

---

snake stopper (snayk stop pur) *n.*
A poop that's long and curvy enough to block its way down the toilet funnel when being flushed.

The longer you look at a snake stopper, the more you start to think of the frozen chocolate yogurt you had at the mall food court.

tubba bubba (tuh bah buh bah) *n.*
A little brown floater you find lurking in the toilet even after you flushed it down.

There are likely hundreds of billions of tubba bubbas still lurking in sewage systems worldwide.

Not to be confused with "Hubba Bubba®," the bubblegum from Wrigley® that also won't go all the way down.

---

turd island (turd aih land) *n.*
When you poop so much, it rises above the water level in your toilet.

A turd island is also the real-life embodiment of a poop emoji. For guys like me, it's a proud accomplishment, usually achieved with the help of three pounds of pulled pork, one full bag of shredded cheese, a half bag of tortilla chips, a can of salsa, and some XXXtra hot ghost pepper sauce. (Ask my partner, she will tell you that I'm not joking.)

---

turd topping (turd tawh peen) *n.*
A poop made on top of another poop.

I've done a turd topping when I think I'm finished pooping, but as I'm putting my pants back on, I realize I need to poop right away, again. I'm not yet adventurous enough to make a turd topping when I discover an un-flushed toilet with someone else's poop, however. I wonder if that makes me a poop prude? Whatever, I won't do sloppy shitty seconds.

VIPeer (vee i péer) *n.*
Someone who checks their phone while at a stand-up urinal.

I also refer to VIPeers as "messytaskers" and "piddlediddlers." I wonder what's so important that it's worth risking peeing all over yourself, or dropping your phone in the urinal?

AND NOW, AN ORIGINAL POOP POEM

This is from a former townhome neighbor, written while he was bored at work. Like me, he was peeved at how some of our neighbors would let their dogs crap anywhere and not clean up after them.

My dear puppy, have you pooped today?
If you haven't, then that's OK.
After you poop, you'll feel good.
Come, let's walk around the hood.
I don't have to poop. You will see.
But I'll go, if not to pee.
Now, here we are at this park.
Still no urge. SQUIRREL!!! BARK! BARK!
Here we are, at this tree.
Take a sniff. You will see.
This spot is perfect for other dogs.
Not for me. I hear frogs.
How about here, on the grass.
I'm a princess. I must pass.

Please poop here, at this shrub.
Not on your life, bub.
We've come full circle at the clubhouse.
I don't think so. See that mouse?
How about here, at the lake?
NO! There's a snake.
You'll feel better. You will see.
Please go here. Please go, for me.
I will not poop at the lake.
A poop here, I will not take.
I will not poop at the clubhouse.
I just can't do it 'cause of the mouse.
I will not poop on the grass.
There is no where to hide my... bum.
I will not poop with other dogs.
I will not dodge others' logs.
Please, please poop for me.
You'll feel better. You will see.
Well, fine then. Here looks good.
I think I'll go. I think I should.
I'll just go here behind this tree.
I do feel better. I feel free.
I do feel better. You were right.
Now I wait while you pack it up tight.
In that small plastic bag tied to my leash.
Can we go home now? I need to sleep.
I'm sorry I doubted you.
You were right all along.
You know what I needed.
I admit it. I was wrong.
The next time we walk the Greenway loop—
I promise, daddy...
I'll go poop.

Pretty impressive poop-pooch-poetry, would you agree? His name is Chris Skidmore and he's a "Dr. Poop Seuss" if you ask me!

GRANTASMS GIVE YOU THE SHITS WITH GIGGLES!

PARTU DEUX

(HOW TO GRANTASM)

Ready, play, Grantasms!

Get ready to be splattered all over with my un-secret sauce! Well, I mean, here's the meaty recipe for how I come up with my Grantasms. (There are no hard instructions here—mix up the order any way you like.)

START WITH YOUR NAME

All words are designed to make things understood. (Well, the good ones are.) What you want to do first is make that connection to yourself. You must wish to *be* understood—recognizable, familiar, known. I'm not talking about being popular; I'm just talking about sharing yourself with those who matter to you.

You don't need to call them "Grantasms"—call them whatever you want, and give it your personal style and flair! Actually, I'd *rather* you called them something else that describes your own identity. Maybe it's a name you've already come up with for the part of you that's quirky, or quippy, or any -y. That's how you remember them, and that's how you *are* remembered (in a good way.)

Don't worry if you can't come up with a name for them, yet! Once you get in the mindset of how each made-up, twisted word relates to yourself, your name for them will come as naturally as it has for me.

Now that you have that mindset, you're ready to start with your social wordplay. My best Grantasms mix three ingredients: creativity, story, and conversation.

INGREDIENT #1: CREATIVITY

Create an original idea to your word or words—be it the word itself, its meaning, or the story behind it. You can even use someone else's word, or their made-up word and description, as long as you give your unique take on it.

I like to define this kind of creativity as **novelty plus value.** It's novel (i.e., something new) which perks our interest, and it's valuable because it gets people laughing and talking. A creative person is an intriguing person. When you create and share, with openness, authenticity, and a willingness to be vulnerable, you gain a better sense of self; you also build confidence and charisma.

INGREDIENT #2: STORY

One thing a Grantasm should always include is an original story (and preferably, your own.) Whether it's a memory from an actual experience, a keen observation or a wild imagination, a happy or difficult time, it should carry some personal meaning and be genuine to who you are. As I learned from Brené Brown, when you allow yourself to be vulnerable, and open with your feelings, your stories start to gel and they spew forth, naturally.

Word creations are the best way I know how to tell a memorable and entertaining story you can connect with most anyone. Many of these Grantasms are my creative outbursts inspired by funny, relatable, and entirely true stories from people I've conversed with—in person as well as online. That makes excellent sense when you consider that *humans have always been wired for stories.*

Grantasms are like having a bunch of easy-to-remember micro-stories in your back pocket, ready to share for any planned or spontaneous opportunity. (Mind you, these aren't something you need to remember verbatim. They're merely here to help bring to the surface the personal stories you already have percolating.)

INGREDIENT #3: CONVERSATION

This is where we build social connections and *get people talking*. If you really want the full power and joy from Grantasms, you must feel comfortable (or courageous) to share your word-story with others. Pick something that feels true to you, and share it with a friend. When you are confident enough, try it with someone you've never met before, or who you know isn't like you, personality-wise. You'll be amazed at the social connections you can make that you may not have thought possible.

All of the Grantasms in this book are ideal to use as conversation practice for all kinds of familiar social settings and in icebreaker situations. I selected these out of *hundreds* of my twisted words that I've had the most conversational success with for an eclectic range of social circumstances: work, dating, eating and drinking, networking professionally and recreationally, chatting online and in person, and our bodily functions. They're for situations from the standard to the insane, and everywhere in between—truly great icebreaker fun!

WANT YOUR GRANTASMS SPICIER? ADD HUMOR

A Grantasm ideally has an element that is amusing and gets people smiling and laughing, so they become more open with you.

Why humor? Because **laughter is one of our best ways to overcome social anxiety and awkwardness.** Humor creates a natural opening for a healthy conversation with someone. In the middle of laughter, you see people connect. It can simply be observational humor, playfully self-deprecating, or a wild point-of-view. The best humor with Grantasms is something therapeutic or adds some levity—and again, gets people talking.

SHOW SOME CARE

Not every Grantasm needs to be comical, especially when you're talking about a sensitive subject or in a sensitive situation. (Otherwise, that would increase the social awkwardness.) That's why it's important to *be always mindful of social context* —who your audience is, how people are feeling, how you're feeling, etcetera. Comedy works best in conversation when you understand context and demonstrate empathy. This is also referred to as emotional intelligence.

With Grantasms you get to practice creative fitness, which builds up your emotional *strength*.

TIPS FOR WHEN YOU'RE FEELING STUCK

Having trouble coming up with new words on your own? Here are some things to try that I've found will make you more likely to get un-stuck and be successful with your word creations...

SOMETHING BORROWED WITH SOMETHING NEW

Here's something fun to try as an exercise: Take an existing, commonly used word and come up with a new description for it. Here's an example:

rock star (rawk star) *n.*

A job description with an ego-boosting name demanding high-level qualifications and experience, to distract from a poverty-level wage offer.

Creativity is not only making up a twisted word; it's the twisted meaning you infuse into it. Bonus points and an extra slice of pie for you if you can come up with more than one twisted description for the same word!

Okay, I don't have anything to offer for bonus points. Do you need my permission to eat more pie, anyway?

WORK IN ONE OF YOUR OWN STORIES

I call this, "something borrowed for something YOU." If you're struggling with coming up with a creative word or a description for it, not to worry. Take any of the words in this book (or have a friend share *their own* made-up word and description), and use that to share a story about yourself that ties into that same word. It's more than just a creative prompt for story-sharing; it's also very therapeutic.

"By **sharing a story** with a supportive audience, either in conversation or in writing, it frees the storyteller of unneeded physical and emotional stress caused by holding the story inside and worrying about it. Brené Brown explains that it helps people to share stories instead of numbing pain with unhealthy choices."

~JENNIFER LYNNE BIRD

Double bonus points and a free round of drinks if you can get someone else to share their story as well!

Did you remember what I just said, earlier? You're responsible for treating everyone to drinks, by the way. ;-)

FIND A BUDDY

Find a friend or group of people that you enjoy socializing with and try this game: Give each other a setting or description, perhaps include a personal anecdote, and challenge each other to come up with a made-up word for it. Do it in a place where you feel most accepted and can be yourself. That may be at a pub, a book club, a game night, a park, or a walk in the woods.

Can't get together in person? Online is also fine, and phone or webcam is better than plain chat. Still, face-to-face is always best, so take the opportunity to make it a "wordplay date"— meet with someone for story-sharing, whenever and wherever you can.

ALWAYS KEEP AN OPEN MIND

Any way you slice it, mix it, shred it, bake it, communicate it— I promise you'll come up with something creative if you always remember to keep an open mind to all the possibilities, including the ones that may seem "stupid" at first.

Don't be afraid of being called that word, either. Stupid is what seems shocking to some who aren't used to something so different, twisted, and creative that connects brains, emotions, and humans in strange and exciting ways.

"There's real power in starting something stupid."

~RICHIE NORTON, AUTHOR OF "THE POWER OF STARTING SOMETHING STUPID."

Remember this: **Grantasms is the game where un-real words create real connections.** Everyone wins for trying, and we all enjoy each other's savory word dishes. It's a pot-luck conversation cookout.

READY TO DIG IN?
LET'S MUNCH ON SOME GRANTASM STORIES!

PARTY TRE

(GRANTASMS STORIES)

Who's got a Grantasm? These folks!

"Being vulnerable is the key to story sharing."

~BRANDON TELIG

Storytelling is fun. As I mentioned in the previous chapter, I like *story sharing* even better.

I'd now like to share some real-life examples from other memorable people in my life. Each of them has a fun and fresh perspective on how they use their own twisted words: for laughs, compelling stories, prompts for attention-grabbing things they might want to sell or promote, help people better understand our shared experiences and personal choices, a memorable way to get their point across, or just "because."

"SPOUSISH"—CELEBRATE NON-TRADITIONAL RELATIONSHIPS

Of course, I'll start with my **Karen**.

Karen and I have been together for ten years. We celebrated with a promise ceremony between just the two of us back in April 2011 very close to my birthplace: the island Oahu, Hawai'i on Waikiki Beach.

Karen would feel socially awkward trying to explain to her family and friends that we are in a serious committed relationship (hopefully one for the rest of our lives), but we choose right now to not be "married," in a legal sense. We didn't want to call ourselves "boyfriend and girlfriend," because that didn't sound as committed, but we weren't spouses, either.

For years, we searched for the perfect word to describe our special relationship. She read books on unmarried couples for creative inspiration, and tried out different words with others in similar relationships.

One day, Karen came up with "**spousish.**" Here's how she explained it to me.

"Spousish was easily understood by most people around me without the awkward list of questions that usually followed. When are you getting engaged? Why not? Who wouldn't want to be married? Don't you want kids? Aren't you married by common law anyway? One single word somehow eliminated the list of questions and was accepted as 'good enough.'"

What a creative solution! Karen and I love to see people's reactions when we tell them we're **spousish**. It's certainly more comfortable for her relatives to wrap their minds around. Sometimes it's also the beginning of a joyful conversation with someone who's no longer a stranger.

One of my book editors later shared with me this story when she was on Christmas vacation...

"I referred to a couple's relationship as "spousish" and my new friend LOVED it! Your influence is rippling and rippling."

There are so many un-married couples like us who are happily spousish. It goes to show that a twisted word can be a wonderful way describe your special relationship with someone.

"YOUTILITY"—START A MOVEMENT

©Jay Baer

I've been blessed to know Jay Baer as a wildly successful author, entrepreneur and hall-of-fame speaker since 2011. He's one of the most well-known social media professionals in the world, and one of the most retweeted digital marketers. He's an all-around great family guy and funny wordsmith, who also can rock a plaid suit while hugging a prickly cactus.

In 2013, Jay released his book, *New York Times* and #1 Amazon bestseller: *Youtility: Why Smart Marketing is About*

Help and Not Hype. The book is Jay's own story, along with many other stories of customer care through social marketing. It propelled Jay to greater heights of fame as a speaker and made him a permanent name in the modern marketer's vocabulary. "So the plan with 'Youtility' was always to make it a movement." Jay explained to me. "I'd be lying to say I wasn't surprised to say it actually worked. 'Youtility' is the only time I've ever made up a word but I pay attention to titles. It matters!"

Here's more Jay had to say about that:

"I fought long and hard with the book publisher about my title. Because, of course, 'Youtility' is not a real word, and they thought that was crazy.

They were like, 'Why don't you call this book, "Useful Content Marketing?"' And I'm like, because, there's no 'there,' there. That's not a movement! There are lots of books that are titled something like that, and that's not terribly interesting.

So by creating a label for it, and to be consistent with the application of that label, and then having extensions of the concept in a lot of different places—there's podcasts, there's blogs or videos —it's allowed to take on a life of its own."

Jay's book publisher wanted something literal and direct, something that might have some heavily searched keywords in the title to put it first with the search engines. But I know Jay. What makes him so successful is not that that he's a marketing genius; he is also a very compassionate guy. Doing a book that lacked any emotional resonance in the title? That would not be him.

Youtility is different. It's catchier than a straightforward title would ever be, and it generated massive word-of-mouth marketing. Jay's success with the book sales, speaking engagements, and revenue from *Youtility* proved that **sharing a twisted word gets your audience's attention.**

If you know how to tell relatable stories and can relate to their feelings and struggles like Jay's book does, you've built an emotional connection and now also have their loyalty for your future endeavors. (That is most certainly true for Jay, as his subsequent books, including his latest one with yet another word creation in the title, *Talk Triggers,* are all best-sellers.)

I can relate to Jay's situation. While I was writing this book, a well-known and respected book consultant told me I should omit the word "Grantasms" in my book title and replace it with "Conversation Starters."

(Ugh, I thought.)

The consultant's argument was the same as Jay's publisher's, which would make sense from a seemingly practical marketing standpoint. Yes, the word-combo of "conversation starters" shows up high in suggested searches on Amazon, and practically no one has ever heard of a "Grantasm," much less searching for it.

I do understand all about search algorithms, having worked in the search engine optimization industry for a decade (yes, really). But I also would think, isn't that a short-term mentality for what's supposed to be a long-term goal?

Jay's story reminded me that ultimately the point of why we

both write our books is connecting with humans, first. Granted, he and I still both included some key search terms in the later portion of our title, but that's by design—to clarify what's now got your attention.

Jay's astounding success with *Youtility* is all the proof you need that if you're looking to start a movement, twisted words are a great way to capture someone's attention and interest towards building an engaged following. It's like that quote I mentioned earlier from Sally Hogshead: **different is better than better;** creating something twisted is far more resonant than copying something familiar.

And guess what, it's also great for search engine optimization (SEO) value, too! The massively successful online marketer, Chris Brogan, mentioned this ten years after he and his co-author, Julien Smith, published their New York Times and Wall Street bestseller, *Trust Agents.* The secret to successful organic traffic and conversions in the search results? It's simple: **come up with your own words.**

"Julien wrote about how creating your own keywords was a much better way to win at SEO instead of competing with existing words. He pointed out that if you could earn enough media attention for a phrase you coined, all roads would naturally point back to your site. I've been using this trick since 2009 and if you look at the traditional SEO markers of my site, it stinks, but I have massive authority around all the terms I created for myself."

CHRIS BROGAN

©Ann Handley

Ann Handley is a *Wall Street Journal* best-selling business author whose had her books translated into nine freakin' languages. She is also a popular keynote speaker at digital marketing conferences and a monthly columnist for *Entrepreneur* magazine. Forbes cites her as the most influential woman in social media and is recognized by ForbesWoman as one of the top 20 women bloggers. I'm also a big fan of her book, *Everybody Writes: Your Go-To Guide to Creating Ridiculously Good Content.*

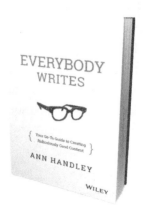

Back in November 2017, Ann was a featured keynote speaker at The Internet Summit conference near me in Raleigh, North Carolina. I had already registered to attend the conference, so I reached out to her on Facebook, and we became "virtual" friends.

Here's a true story—Ann and I were having our lunch break at a conference. We were standing over a small circular standing table, just 3 feet from each other, eating in total silence and without ever saying a word to each other the entire time. Why? We didn't recognize each other! I did think it was possible that this person facing me *was* Ann Handley, but we were so far into eating our lunches in silence that breaking the silence seemed weird.

Sure enough, right after lunch in a packed crowd at the keynote ceremony, who should get up on stage but that very same woman I ate lunch "at," but not really "with"—how funny, right? Of course, being that we were Facebook friends, how could I *not* mention this to Ann after the conference?

To my pleasant surprise, Ann shared a funny and poignant word about our socially awkward experience.

"Preunion."

"LOL, I think we both didn't realize who each other was! No problem, totally cool :) It was nice to see you, and I'm glad we realized it after the fact! We never met, but we knew each other. Preunion—also, not my word —Scott Monty gets credit for it!"

~*Ann Handley*

Because of that, I also reached out to Scott Monty to hear more of his story, and we ended up being Facebook friends as well. (I later learned "preunion" was in one of our standard English dictionaries.)

Ann's and Scott's stories reminded me of how, during my research and vetting of all my own made-up words in this very book, which I *thought* were originals, *had already been mentioned elsewhere in some form*. Maybe we had different implied meanings (or perhaps very similar ones), but it's always our personal and relatable stories that make them fresh and unique to each of us. That's especially true when we hear them for the first time, or come up with them on our own. **Our stories are the ships and anchors to our word discoveries.**

Here's how a friend of mine put it to me after I shared with her this very story:

"Yes! I thought the same with my made-up words. I liked to think I used them so much that others caught on, but I should know better!"

It shows that a creative made-up word can originate from someone else, and still be used for alleviating any feelings of social awkwardness after a meeting (including a preunion), then weaved into a story that is entirely yours.

"GRUNCHING"—BE MORE DISTRACTION-FRIENDLY

©Rick Green

Rick Green is a full-time comedian, and the producer and director at Big Brain Productions/Totally ADD out of Toronto, Canada. He's written and performed in over 700 television and radio programs and co-authored the best-selling book, *ADD Stole My Car Keys: The Surprising Ways Adult Attention Deficit Disorder Affects Your Life... and Strategies for Creating a Life You Love.*

This book is perhaps the funniest (and certainly one of the most relatable) I've read on ADHD. I highly recommend for spouses and family members who want to understand a loved one with ADHD much better.

Rick and his wife, Ava, are also the co-founders of the popular website for ADHD folks, TotallyADD.com. Rick is also a recipient of the prized "Order of Canada," which I guess is a medal that someone high up in Canada hangs around your neck for doing decades of bizarre stuff, like Rick has. (Or maybe, to get you to stop?)

Seriously though, I discovered Rick and Ava in 2011 when I chanced across a groundbreaking documentary playing on the PBS station in Chicago, where I used to live: *ADD and Loving It?!*, produced and hosted by the couple. (Well, Rick did all of the talking on camera, of course—he's the one with ADHD.)

I only recently learned that Rick also loves making up words and sharing his personal stories behind them, which he refers to as his "Rickisms." Here's is one of his favorites:

Grunching—Singing a tune by grunting the melody.

> "[Grunching] came from a skit I wrote many years ago in which a scroat (a term of abuse for a despised or despicable person), played by me, named Timmy Target, arrives on the doorstep of an upscale home to deliver a Grunt-A-Gram. The woman is baffled. My character explains that it's like a singing telegram, only I grunt it. I then proceed to do a very off-key version of 'Happy Birthday' while snorting like a constipated rhino who desperately wants to meet a lady rhino. It's funnier than it sounds."
>
> ~RICK GREEN

For people with ADHD like Rick and myself, making up words and sharing our true personal stories is a way to harness our crazy random thoughts into something focused that can make us better storytellers, conversation buddies, and relationship partners. (Or at least, slightly less aggravating ones.)

Even people who aren't on the ADHD spectrum get the benefits, since we all get distracted sometimes. Just some of us do way, *way* more than others (and with more interesting results).

> "I like making up words because then people mistake me for Shakespeare, who also made up a lot of words (1,700 of them!)"
>
> ~ALSO, RICK GREEN

SO WHAT HAVE WE LEARNED?

I know what I've learned—Rick is delusional. But I also think it's this...

Sharing our twisted words helps us "get" each other, and ourselves. They connect us to the stories we want to remember and share, like we're hearing them for the first time ourselves even when we tell them again and again. They make us laugh and get us talking, including with people that might seem very different from us on the surface. They certainly attract likeable and like-minded people, and assure us that we are not alone.

With my intimate partner, friends, colleagues, and even passing acquaintances, Grantasms brings us together. They certainly help us understand each other better, which is impressive in itself when trying to stand out from the fog and the noise. They help us enjoy the good parts about being "different" and appreciate what all have in common, and can all share—our personal and relatable stories from twisted words.

Share your own twisted words—that's the formula for spectacular social health. Twisted words leads to conversations, and conversations lead to connections, and connections are what we're *all* craving.

GRANTASMS ARE CREATIVE CRAVING WITH STORY SHARING!

My twisted ADHD story (like, really, really twisted)

Now that I've shared others' stories with twisted words, I'm ready to share with you my own. Trust me, it's like really twisted. I'm talking pretzel-y, balloon-animaly twisted.

MY STRUGGLE WITH DISTRACTION...

and impulsivity, and managing my emotions, and going on tangents, and—oh, what's that?

For most of my life, I had a gift I didn't know how to unwrap, or open without breaking the present inside.

You already know I'm talking about Attention Deficit Hyperactivity Disorder (ADHD). Surprisingly, it's still not as well-understood as you might think. A lot of people think it's something everyone deals with occasionally, rather than understanding it for what it is: a developmental disorder.

A disorder isn't necessarily bad when you know what you have and how to harness it; it can even be an advantage. But when you *aren't* aware of what you have or how to properly deal with it, your life falls apart. It's like having pieces of a puzzle that don't seem to fit, and only break into more pieces every time you try.

I WAS A SOCIAL KLUTZ

Growing up, I was painfully unsuccessful in my attempts to have a social life. I got more cold shoulders than warm handshakes.

As a kid, I was socially awkward due to my undiagnosed and untreated ADHD. I missed social cues all the time. I was bullied incessantly and had trouble making and keeping friends. My grades were poor, and my teachers kept telling my parents I had great potential if only "he applied himself."

I AM
trying
harder
(dammit)

What they didn't understand was **I couldn't focus on important things if they were boring.** I tried and tried and tried, but I just couldn't. I found much of what was going on in school to be incredibly dull. Adding to my misery, I would get only part of what the teacher was communicating with the class. It was like I was missing everything third word from whomever was speaking (even worse if it was a noisy environment) and those I did hear would come out strange sometimes. I was like I need a translator for a language that even I couldn't describe.

I was clueless, utterly hopeless, and got beaten up *a lot*. Many times at night, I wondered if some evil spirit was coming into my room while I was sleeping and poisoning me with something? As crazy as that sounds, it would at least explain why I felt cursed.

HITTING ROCKITY BOTTOM

Well into adulthood, I was still missing cues. My attention and memory were always deficient. No matter how hard I tried to follow along, I would find myself forgetting how to approach things. I'd get easily distracted before, during, and after most conversations. Often my emotions got the better of me; I lost job opportunities, clients, relationships, and even my physical health.

In 2001, a sleep study center diagnosed me with one of the worst cases of sleep apnea they had ever seen. If you have sleep apnea your breathing stops during sleep; not only do you go about your day sleep deprived, but your vital organs like your brain, heart, and lungs are deprived of oxygen. Yes, sleep apnea is one slow killer.

zzzzzzzzzzzzzCRASH!

Yes, crash. I crashed my car twice because I'd fall asleep at the wheel. I was extremely fortunate both times, having already slowed down as I was approaching my townhome residence, but my brain hit the snooze button before I could park my car, so I crashed into a tree on the opposite side of the road both times. Poor tree.

SO I CHECKED MYSELF, BUT...

The first time I tried getting help, it didn't go well.

I was 33 years old when a psychiatrist diagnosed me with severe ADHD. At the time I was married to a woman with

132

equally challenging personal issues, and she wasn't able to support me with mine. I still remember her anger when she learned of my diagnosis...

"It's not fair, you're the one who's supposed to be taking care of ME!" she complained.

Yeah, how selfish of me to have ADHD, right?

The psychiatrist first prescribed me Ritalin, but it made me feel like a robot. I asked to try a different drug, so they put me on Adderall, not much better. After about a month, I confided with my then-wife that while I could focus, I was feeling way more anxious and not at all my creative self anymore.

"That's how 'normal' people feel all the time," she responded dismissively. So, was I selfish to expect *any* understanding? Normal people couldn't feel as "off" as I was feeling, could they?

I saw my psychiatrist again, who took me off the meds. But the problems in my marriage and my overall life persisted. I was increasingly unhappy, feeling stuck working at my home business that was going nowhere. I craved social connection, but I was also living in the boonies of Illinois, with no one locally I could relate to.

My un-life sucked.

GOING UNDER THE KNIFE

In late 2005, I was now going through a divorce and living on my own. I decided to have invasive surgery for my sleep apnea, which had become life-threatening. Can you imagine going through your life having ADHD and sleep apnea at the same time? Picture a lack of oxygen to your brain, compounded by the synapses in your brain already struggling to connect critical information.

The surgery was a success. Finally, I could breathe—literally.

Early next year, I got divorced. I could breathe again—figuratively.

A FRESH START

I had just turned 39 when I found a loving and supportive partner who could see through all my personal shit; she pushed me to modify my self-destructive behavior.

It would take me until I was 41 to find a medication that worked. It didn't cure anything, mind you. It just made me self-aware of the issues I had, and now I could see what I had to do. I made the big jump of filing for personal bankruptcy and getting out from under my business that I'd struggled with for over ten years. It was just what I needed so badly for so long—a fresh start.

With a stronger foundation, I realized that if I was ever going to reach my goals, I needed to do something about my lingering problems. Medication alone wasn't going to solve it. I needed to train myself how to focus, remember the important stuff, think in an orderly sequence, pick up social cues, manage my emotions, and communicate better.

But first, I had to figure out how I'd learn and do all of that—successfully. You know, be consistent, make it stick. Then one day it hit me:

What if I turned my struggles into a game?

DISCOVERING MY GIFT

After a few years of mild successes on my own with cognitive behavior therapy and a coaching group for adults with ADHD, I discovered that I seemed to do much better when I treated struggles as part of a playful game. I also realized that the one game that seem to always work best was this:

Come up with word creations, share them in appropriate social situations with different people, and listen to everyone's stories.

Grantasms—twisted words and meanings for telling my stories—helped me transform my ADHD from a curse into a gift. I could now flip a frustration into a creation, and use it to have a fulfilling conversations with new people for warm connections. The social connections improved my mental connections, and vice-versa.

PAUSE IS POWERFUL

"What we pay attention to grows. The challenge is the most dominant thoughts we have tend to be negative."

~DAVID GIWERC, PRESIDENT OF ADD
COACH ACADEMY

David reminds me that the "pause is power," especially for folks with ADHD. David explained to me that a lot of our struggles come from failing to pause—i.e., to slow down and pay attention to when we may be having negative thoughts. As a result, we are unconsciously letting those thoughts dominate the emotional center of our brain (aka, the limbic system), and thus taking over from the rational side of our mind.

For someone who doesn't have the cognitive ability to pay proper attention to either their emotional state or their social environment, these chemicals cause us to instinctively react overly negative, fearful, even hostile, to situations where we perceive some threat to our social being. We understand this as feeling social anxiety.

Before Grantasms, I would often blurt out whatever was in my head, without being mindful of social context. I never realized how badly I would come across.

Grantasms put me in a "game master" mindset, so to speak. Many games aren't just about competition, they're also designed as social opportunities. Now when I'm in social situations, I think of them like a game. Grantasms make me pause and be more aware before I speak. I am now more mindful of myself and intentional with my choices for communication— i.e., original words and phrases—that are relevant and appropriate for the situation. Sure, they can be funny or an opportunity to find the humor in; more importantly, they're meant to show that you're listening and you care about who you're talking with.

AN ADHD GAME-CHANGER

Grantasms are one of the best things I've done to manage my ADHD; they play to my strengths and control my weaknesses. With Grantasms I've sharpened my skills, become a better listener, and gotten the right things done. It also makes me more aware of the personal growth of others who do it as well, and validate their feelings and accomplishments.

CREATIVE EMPATHY

Sometimes I refer to Grantasms as "creative empathy" for managing my ADHD, perhaps because I love to make others laugh and have a good time while doing it. I know one of the gifts of having ADHD is it has also made me more empathetic to people who also have to deal with overwhelming distractions and missed social cues, no matter where they may fall on the spectrum.

ADHD is still a daily struggle, but I'm now more willing to face new struggles as a growth opportunity rather than a reminder of any perceived disability. It has helped me discover my greatest gift and reward—discovering my personal story and sharing genuine social connections with wonderful people that wouldn't have been possible, otherwise.

I'm blessed to have a lifelong opportunity ahead of me, to share some laughs with new people and get each other talking— both ADHD and non-ADHD folks—over our twisted words.

To me, that's "Grantastic."

That ain't really a real word (ain't it?)

My partner, Karen, told me her high school teachers berated her for using the word "ain't." They claimed it was an improper word, yet we already know it had been used commonly, everywhere, for many decades.

"AREN'T THOSE JUST FAKE WORDS?"

That's still something I hear from people without imagination.

Isn't that what some of our teachers, family members, or peers used to tell us? Sometimes they scoff at us for doing so? Or maybe, they still do?

AREN'T YOU GOING TO PISS OFF SOME PEOPLE?

Yes, a few I already have. Most of the feedback is usually positive or politely indifferent. However, I've come across hyper-analytical control freaks at different meetups who have gotten offended—yes, *offended*—just at the though of creating and sharing made-up words.

I remember it well: one instance was with a group conversation that included a search engine optimization (SEO) coder. He became so worked up over hearing some of my made-up words that he raised his voice in disgust, while his hand shook tremendously and spilled beer all over our table.

"Entrypreneur?! That's too different from entrepreneur!"

Yes, I had changed one letter, and that alone was offensive to him. This from a guy who works in the search engine industry known for made-up words like "Google" and "Bing." (I didn't say that his response was rational.)

Another time, I happened to be next to a lab scientist at a writing meetup. I remember so vividly her discomfort as I shared the theme of my book, which she scowled disapprovingly and said, without any hint of irony...

"I don't think that just words matter all that much."

Again, this happened at a *writing meetup*.

THE STRANGULATION OF COMMUNICATION

Control freaks want to strangle creative communication. I accepted that a long time ago. Their mindset of what's "real" is entirely unreal to me. Ironically, any standard dictionary still has a multitude of words in it that are so archaic; these same naysayers would swear that *those* aren't real words if they ever heard them spoken out loud.

HOW DO THEY KNOW WHAT'S REAL, REALLY?

So, what did I do? I *grantasm'd.*

I turned their dark energy into light energy through my creativity game. Every time I received negative feedback or felt like I wasn't being understood or taken seriously, I took it as a creative challenge for myself. I'd train myself to come up with a new word about my frustration with these people, diffuse their criticisms, and laugh about it. I even made it part of my own identity.

nayslayer (neigh sleigh ur) *n.*
Someone who has fun with naysayers by playfully diffusing their argument.

NAYSLAYING THE NAYSAYERS

So if anyone is ever skeptical about your new word creation, Here's a convincing way to explain it as a valuable form of communication:

- You have an original definition and a personal story to share with it.
- You say it in context with an existing situation or conversation.
- You get others to talk about it, and share it on their own.

SÎ PABLO, ALL WORDS ARE "MADE UP"

That is my best nayslayer argument for why you can (and should) make up your own words and share them. Remember all the words we have are made up by someone, somewhere, sometime. The words you came up with on your own, or heard someone claim they came up with—those too probably were already thought of by someone else, beforehand.

A lot of words that have been around for centuries that we like to believe were our "own" were borrowed from other cultures and languages. Many had their own meanings transformed or pronunciations altered, to stay relevant to the time and culture. Not all of them stuck throughout history, obviously. But through them we learn so much more about our history.

Words that were once considered slang (like "OK") became mainstream. When they became overused, they evolved to be fun to say in a different way, and still relevant in the same way (e.g., "okily dokily" and "okee dokee.")

That's why making up new words is essential for healthy communication. Besides...

A DICTIONARY IS A GUIDE, NOT HARD SCIENCE

Standardized dictionaries are all products of their time. Some words stay with us and become timeless, and sure, they'll always add more with each new yearly version. It's also true that dictionaries are full of words that are unused and irrelevant to most of us. They may be useful for a historical understanding, but they aren't practical for most of our modern conversations.

WORD EXPERTS AGREE—MAKE UP THOSE WORDS

Professional lexicographers attest that many words we use today, you won't find in any standard dictionary. The words in our modern dictionaries—some which are many centuries old—must've been made up by someone, somewhere, right?

(I sometimes wonder, do most Americans realize that most of their chosen English words derived from other languages?)

SO, WHAT MAKES A WORD, REAL?

Of course, the UrbanDictionary.com website was created for just that—crowdsourcing new words, or existing words with creative new meanings (both descriptions and use examples), and voting up or down on them, with an award bestowed on the "top definition."

To me, what makes a word "real" is not if it's accepted and published into a standard dictionary, it's about whether it's still relevant and used effectively in our conversation *when being our genuine selves.*

Real (reel) *n.*

1. Existing as a thing or occurring in fact; not imagined or supposed.
2. **True, genuine.**

To comprehend what's real, you should first understand what's authentic about human nature. Authentic people are willing to express what they feel. People who dare to do that, to show their vulnerable side, and do it in a way that is unique to who they are and speaks to who they are, are creative individuals.

What makes these creative individuals seem *even more real* to others—when they strive to connect with other people and be part of a community.

WORDS ARE INVENTIONS (AND RE-INVENTIONS)

What also makes a word "real" is the genuine experience that births them, and others can relate. Words are born from shared experience; new, shared experiences transform those same words—new pronunciations, new derivations, even adopted into foreign languages!

Any linguist will tell you that words and language are fluid means of communication, not stagnant. Their meanings change over time; they evolve as our cultures evolve. So many words we commonly use today, such as "google" or "tweet" (both of which can be a noun or a verb), were never words until someone was creative enough, and open enough, to share them.

That's why we need a creative process for getting the words out of us to express what we personally, genuinely mean.

URBANDICTIONARY.COM: RISQUÉ, BUT NOT ALWAYS RELATABLE

A twisted word with an interesting meaning isn't all that memorable without a compelling story, and it's less likely to stick if you don't even know who's the storyteller.

UrbanDictionary.com is the most popular crowdsourced word site today. It's a fun site and can offer some creative inspiration. However, it doesn't allow you to see the actual identities of the word creators. There are no descriptive profile pages, like you would get for an Amazon author bio. Can you remember the handle of someone in there who shared a made-up word or phrase you liked? Could you ever reach out to them and have a conversation with them about it? Could you even start or join a conversation thread?

No, you can't. That's done intentionally by design. There is nothing about it that is genuinely social, and that's our problem.

UrbanDictionary.com is a popular site regularly flowing with made-up words, and the business model is built around amazingly search-engine discoverable, quick-and-fun info with casual involvement. But it is entirely without any opportunity for real connection.

WHAT WE NEED OUR WORDS TO SAY

I know today, many of us crave more of our words to have a genuine social connection.

I want to know the person who created the word and the story behind it, don't you? I want to share my words, and other peoples' words I can relate to, along with the actual stories behind them. I want also to hear the stories of other word creators and converse with them.

I need my made-up words to have shared meaning and shared bonds. I want to know there's a human being with a name and a personality and a history to remind me that I'm not alone. I want my words to comfort someone else and remind them that they're not alone; we get each other.

That's not too much to ask of our own words, is it?

GRANTASMS HELP YOU FEEL CONNECTIONS!

Fighting filler-flabber (unsuck those words!)

filler-flabber (fill ur flah bur) *n.*
Overuse of filler words so drastic that it distracts from the important content, creates distrust, and drives others crazy.

*You don't notice them until you do, and then you can't stop noticing them? Words such as "like," "right," "awesome," "absolutely," "totally," "whatchamacallit," "um," "okay," "yeah," and our most contagious filler-word today, **"y'know."***

MY FILLER-FLABBER STORY

July 2017—a day I just returned home from my partner's dad's funeral.

RIIIINNNNNGGGG!

(Okay, that's not how my cell phone rang, but you get the idea.)

"Hi, is this Grant?"

It was a female voice, I guessed early-to-mid-twenties, and very perky.

"Yes, who's calling?" I asked.

"Hey, Grant! How are you doing?"

"Okay, who is this?" I asked. (I still get peeved by cold call introductions with fake familiarity.)

"Oh, I'm 'so-and-so' with 'such-and-such recruiting agency!' We saw your resume on one of the online job boards, so I was calling to see if you might be interested in a full-time position with a company which we think you'd be perfect for! So, how are you doing today?"

"Not good, unfortunately," I replied. "I just returned from a funeral."

*"Oh, **awesome!**"*

"Huh?? I don't think that's really awesome?"

*"Oh, yeah, sorry about that! Just being friendly, **y'know**! So, Grant, I have your resume in front of me, and I see you have a lot of really great work experience! I'd like to submit you out to some of the companies we partner with, and I just need to enter some information in our database, first. So, could you please tell me how you spell your last name just so I can confirm our info?"*

"Um, okay? It's C-R-O-W-E-L-L."

"*Perfect!*..."

That was perfect, really?

I wonder why people say this after you give them the spelling of your name. Would it have been imperfect if I only had one letter "l" in my name? Or removed the "e?" Would any other response have made her say, "Oh, I'm sorry?"

What do I get for such perfection, anyway? Or maybe, was she complimenting herself? Did she struggle with typing or something?

"What's this job opening you think I'm such a good fit for?" I asked.

"We don't actually have any job openings for you right now. But we'll be sure to let you know when something opens up!"

"Well, why did you—"

*"Hey **y'know**, in the meantime, it really would be **awesome** if you could 'Friend' us and 'Like' us on Facebook, **y'know**? Can you also connect with me on LinkedIn? That way you can find out about all of our future job openings and submit your resume again."*

"Again? I never submitted my resume to you guys. You said you got mine off of a job site."

*"Yeah, **y'know**, I get it, it's cool! And if we're connected on LinkedIn you can do it right away when we do have something! One more thing, can you tell me what other jobs you're applying for and how much you made at your last—"*

CLICK.

Ok, being totally transparent, I exaggerated this story after the "perfect" part. (I'm just sharing how I was playing it back in my mind after the call.)

A GRANTASM KEPT ME CALM AND CREATIVE

Well, calm enough. Looking back on my experience with this recruiter, I can see it was a profound case of filler-flabber—how we often make words meaningless by our overuse, misuse, and abuse of them.

When we aren't really paying attention to what we're saying, we're also not really paying attention to what the other person is saying. It make us seem uncaring and inconsiderate—even if that's not our intention, it creates a shitty impression.

Whoever said that sticks and stones may break our bones but words will never hurt us, never lived in our social era. (Sticks, really? They must have had fragile bones.)

Now, the old Grant would have likely responded something like this...

"*Y'know*, it would be just so *awesome* if you would remove me from your database and stop calling me with your phony spiel and actually look up the meaning of the word 'perfect.' **Y'know**?!"

PHONE SLAM. NEGATIVE GOOGLE REVIEW. FACEBOOK LIVE RANT. INSTAGRAM-MAD-TAG, YOUTUBE PUBLISH, AND WASTE OF TIME.

Exhausting. Short term gratification for myself doing all that, maybe. But I'd carry around negative residue hindering the rest of my day.

Knowing I had my Grantasms, I was not letting any of her filler-flabber get to me. I was calm, collected, and feeling more like an observer to the situation as it was happening in real-time. I was aware that the conversation was becoming bizarre, yet I realized others must go through this a lot. What an opportunity to play the Grantasms game—I now have a twisted word for that!

LAUGH AT THE BEHAVIOR YOU WANT TO FIX

You can glean from my personal story, **making up words helps me in lots of stressful social situations.** The earlier "me" would have flown off the handle and said or done things I would have later regretted. The new "me" has Grantasms.

I came up with the word *filler-flabber* also a playful reminder to improve *my* use of filler words. For myself and many others, humor is therapeutic and a super-effective way to deal with problems. It puts us in a positive mindset and gives us the satisfaction of a creative accomplishment.

CREATIVE EMPATHY (AGAIN)

Remember what I shared about creative empathy, earlier? A made-up word is also a great prompt for empathizing better. Now when someone else is filler-flabbering, I don't nitpick as much anymore. I think someone like that young woman has made so many calls that she doesn't even know she's coming across like an automaton. It could have just been her feeling nervous, or just trying to stay positive through a stressful work day.

We sometimes do need filler words to keep our sentences together, our thoughts flowing, and for much needed pauses. We need them to get through the stressful parts of life, even the good parts. And when we catch ourselves filler-flabbering, we need Grantasms to allow ourselves to laugh and learn from them.

GRANTASMS GIVE PLAYFUL MEANING TO OUR PROBLEM WORDS (AND DIFFICULT PEOPLE!)

Notsperts
(challenge expertations!)

©R. Gino Santa Maria & ©sumnersgraphicsinc / stock.adobe.com

notspert (not spurt) *n.*
Someone with highly questionable claims of expertise.

WHAT'S AN EXPERT (REALLY)?

"Expert"—it's been a problematic word for me. I know it's meant to label someone as an authority in a field or subject. But I come across so many people who list themselves as experts with little to back it up (or who become defensive when asked).

The word "expert" feeds too much into the ego trips of business people, academics, and self-appointed critics—many of whom decide that they no longer have to step outside of their comfort zone and try learning anything new, especially from anyone who they don't consider to be on their own level.

You know who I'm talking about—dicks.

WHAT MAKES ME THINK I'M "QUALIFIED"...

To talk about words? Well, they're mine.

I don't mean I came up with them all or that nobody else came up with them before me. Indeed, a lot of these words in this book, probably most of them, were said by someone else before me, whom I had no idea about when I first came up with them.

I'm just saying that when I *feel* like I either created them on my own or maybe heard them from somewhere—either consciously or subconsciously—they *connected* with me. When I come up with a twisted description, even with already familiar words like "rockstar" or "amazon," I've now planted the seeds for one of my micro-stories.

The stories? They're mine, too. Either I experienced them first-hand, or I remember where I was when I observed it. Sure, there's some hyperbole with a few of them, but it always feels genuine to who I am; otherwise, I wouldn't feel as connected to them, and they would lose their Grantasm-ness.

"The true sign of intelligence is not knowledge but imagination."

ALBERT EINSTEIN

BEING A TWISTED WORDSMITH "NOTSPERT"

It's much easier to call myself a notspert than an expert on words and communication. You see, I am not an etymologist, a lexicographer, or any other kind of language professional. I don't have any academic background or formal training in this area. I even suck at most standardized wordplay: crossword puzzles, Scrabble, or other favorite word games. Over half of the adult population could probably beat me at any of them.

Squirrel thought: which makes me think about how cool would it be to have Made-Up Word Scrabble? If you could give a plausible definition or share a personal story, you would earn points.

Ok, back to my original thought before I went off on a tangent there... I do have a few things going for me: First, I'm passionate enough about it to talk anyone's ear off about it. Second, some people think I'm funny enough to express it. Third, I care enough to not give a shit and just do it. (Ok, that sounds like a contradiction but I think you know what I mean.)

I've validated through hundreds, maybe thousands of social interactions, that these Grantasms are great communication fun. They also help with remembering important stuff, turning distractions into directions, and just being more pleasant to be around.

It's not a formal study, just my life experience. Because...

YOUR CONNECTIONS ARE YOUR QUALIFICATIONS

We are all "qualified" to share our experiences with our words when they come from our personal, genuine stories. Don't let any so-called expert tell you otherwise, and just "notspert'em" if they do.

GRANTASMS ARE FOR MY FELLOW TWISTED WORDSMITH NOTSPERTS, NEWBIES, AND EVERYONE IN BETWEEN!

Afterword

"I'm not trying to save the world; I just want to leave it better than I showed up. I am funny, too."

~JENNIFER KEYS (MY SASSY FRIEND)

What made me want to write this? Writing made-up stuff based on real stuff in my life? I guess that's what you could call it.

We've heard the saying, there's a book in each of us? Well, forget that. That's a crazy reason to have to be stuck with doing all this friggin' work.

Maybe I did it because I just want your money? Yeah, that's it—stick 'em up. Hand it all over.

Okay, I don't want *all* of your money. You'll need some of it to keep paying me for the many books ahead. And the t-shirts, the calendar, the luxury cruise ship getaway, the major motion picture based on this book with me playing myself, the goat yoga franchise, the 2024 presidential run with trucker caps that read, "Make Grant Rich ~~Again~~ (For the First Time)"

Maybe we can work out a payment plan?

WHY I (REALLY) WROTE THIS BOOK

Yes, seriously now, for real... I created this book because I love making people laugh and talking with each other.

I really think I can make communication fun.

I know that we crave connections, and that a lot of healthy connections come from having fun and meaningful communication. It brings joy to our lives.

I also know (because I've discovered it and have lived it) that a super-creative, empathetic, and successful way to have enjoyable communication is with twisted words.

There you go.

I want you to enjoy my favorite twisted words in this book. Hopefully you'll use them as prompts for your storytelling and conversations, help with remembering the important stuff, and staying emotionally balanced. It certainly has with me and others close to me.

We don't have to go through life continuously distracted, lonely, depressed, misunderstood. We really can get along better than we think. We can make our social interactions with others more humorous, fun, playful, and surprisingly meaningful—with twisted words.

THERE'S REAL POWER...

in the words we create, and more power sharing them. Words shape how we feel, how we put ideas together, and how we get along. Every time we share something creative, we build our identity. We get to know ourselves better as unique individuals. We build strong, emotional connections with *other* individuals and communities, including ones we never realized we were a part of. We discover people that are like us, appreciate and understand people different from us, and celebrate everyone.

FUNNY IS A BEAUTIFUL COMPLIMENT

Just being considered creative and funny is both a joy and an honor. To make others laugh and remember you in a good way? To help them grow, and grow along with them? That's something I feel deep gratitude for being blessed with this gift, which came through my willingness to face my struggles, gain the power to laugh about them and learn from them, and grow from. It is something you can teach to others and feel more connected in the process.

WE'RE NOT ALONE

I now know there are other people all over world like me: We enjoy making up and sharing our twisted words. More than just for laughs and trying to impress people. We believe that it brings us all to a better place.

OUR LANGUAGE CONNECTS US

It's a gift we feel compelled to share with others we care about, or those we want to get along better with, or those we want to handle better next time, *so we don't fly off the handle.*

Words are great for that.

To be able to use our words in a structured way and share our stories is the glue that keeps humans together—couples, groups, teams, tribes, communities, villages, nations—everyone.

SO, WHAT'S STOPPING US?

I believe it stems from our inflexible use of familiar words to communicate what we're thinking.

Today's Americans are less likely than people of any other developed country to be proficient in a second language. Often, Americans don't even agree on the meaning of many of our own words!

Without being able to comprehend that a word can transform its meaning across history, languages, cultures, and time—people become stagnant, and their speech becomes a barrier rather than a bridge to healthy human relationships. That, my friend, is exactly why I'm telling you...

IT'S TIME TO CREATE AND SHARE YOUR TWISTED WORDS

I wrote this book of Grantasms to share the fun in communicating more creatively and openly with anyone, and to make you more relatable to everyone. Words and wordplay are lots of fun for me, but I've realized it's ultimately not the words themselves that connect us, it's the sharing.

That is where face-to-face conversations and genuine relationships happen. It's *truly* social. And, that is why Grantasms (or whatever name you want to give them, maybe with your name) is my necessity for enjoyably productive communication and relationships in our dynamic social era.

MY #1 GOAL FOR YOU...

Share a twisted word.

Share your very first twisted word that speaks to who you are, and a personal story about it with someone whom you can have a conversation. Treat them to lunch, coffee, beer, wine, kombucha, whatever—over a conversation where you can both be yourselves. Listen intently and journal the experience. Plan a date and social event if that will make you commit to it.

My goal is to give you creative inspiration and motivation (and for some, confidence) to share your twisted words—face-to-face, a phone call or video conference, a text chat, a handwritten letter to someone—*anywhere.* Not just with close friends, either —with *everyone* who needs to hear them. (Yes, strangers as well.) That is how you will spread joy, through fun communication.

I HOPE YOU'VE ENJOYED THIS BOOK

Really, I do. Yes, my humor is sometimes sarcastic, and playfully so. I want this book to bring value to your life and I want to hear about it. I hope it's worth reading again and again. This book is a tremendous milestone on my long, bumpy journey of helping us have better conversations and feel more connected. I know we certainly need it.

YOU GET IT, NOW SHARE IT

Accept this as my gift to share with anyone— in face-to-face conversations, storytelling, all kinds of social settings.

In a world of increasing distractions and polarization, we can re-connect with each other through a new take on our shared language, which feels both unique and excitingly familiar—one twisted word at a time.

GRANTASMS IS THE SOCIAL WORD GAME WHERE WE CAN ALL WIN

It's the only word game I know where you can "gerk"—discover your true individual self *and* grow with others for some bigger meaning in our words. The more you share, laugh, and care, the better we all are for it.

"Watch your thoughts; they become words. Watch your words; they become actions. Watch your actions; they become habits. Watch your habits; they become your character. Watch your character; it becomes your destiny."

~LAO-TZU

GET TWISTED TODAY! GO GRANTASMS!

Want more Grantasms?
Of course you do!

FOLLOW ME ON TWITTER & INSTAGRAM:

@yourtwistedwords is where you'll find me sharing a new twisted word, icebreaker help or another creative conversation tip, or just random thoughts that pop into my noggin. (Direct Message if you have a great twisted word of your own to share, or a fantastic resource.)

EMAIL IS GOOD, TOO

Email me at grant@yourtwistedwords.com and please put "Grantasms" in the subject line. Share with me any feedback: what you liked or think could be better, what you'd want to see more of in future books, and any other comments or questions. Of course, I'd love to hear your own stories relatable to any of my twisted words in this book. Or, if you'd like to share some of your own, I can include them in future blog posts on my website, or in my social media. (I always give credit, too.)

SUBSCRIBE TO MY NEWSLETTER

www.yourtwistedwords.com (I like to think the www. stands for Wowee-Wow-Wow.) My goal this year is to deliver a monthly newsletter, always with a new word and engaging story, plus a fun icebreaker tip. You'll also be the first to hear about any new books, fun stuff I have available, and freebies (like an exclusive video series on how to use Grantasms for winning icebreakers.)

MEET ME IN PERSON OR OUT-PERSON (ONLINE)

I'm also available for hire if you're looking for an engaging speaker, workshop leader, or donating soon-to-expire craft beer. Or just say hi, and share a twisted word and your story with me. Let me know if you're traveling through my area in Durham, North Carolina. (We have coffee and pie here, too!)

AUTHOR'S ASK

This book is about the power of creative communication in us all. Your voice determines whether GRANTASMS is successful in helping people express themselves more creatively, have winning conversations, and have loads of fun doing it. So if you like GRANTASMS, please talk about it!

Please review this book on Amazon or whenever you see it available. If you do so online, tag me and/or use the hashtag **#YourTwistedWords.** And if you have a favorite podcast, blogsite, or influencer spot that you think would be a great fit for an interview, please refer them to me as well. (Trust me, I have a good radio voice. :-)

Your review will help others discover this book!

Additional resources

Here are some resources I quote in my book for inspiration. I recommend checking them all out if you'd like to enjoy even more laughs and strong connections!

BOOKS

- *Sniglets* by Rich Hall. (1984-1990, 1994)
- *Faster Than Normal: Turbocharge Your Focus, Productivity, and Success with the Secrets of the ADHD Brain* by Peter Shankman (2017)
- *Youtility: Why Smart Marketing is About Help, Not Hype* by Jay Baer (2013)
- *Talk Triggers: The Complete Guide to Creating Customers with Word of Mouth* by Jay Baer & Daniel Lemin (2019)
- *The Power of Vulnerability: Teaching Authenticity, Connection, and Courage* by Brené Brown, PhD (2013)
- *ADD Stole My Car Keys: The Surprising Ways Adult Attention Deficit Disorder Affects Your Life... and Strategies for Creating a Life You Love* by Rick Green and Umesh Jain (2011)
- *The Power of Starting Something Stupid: How to Crush Fear, Make Dreams Happen, and Live Without Regret* by Richie Norton and Natalie Norton (2013)
- *There is No B2B or B2C: It's Human to Human #H2H* by Brian Kramer

VIDEOS

- *ADD and Mastering It! 36 Strategies That Work! PBS Documentary* (2012)
- *ADD and Loving It?! Award Winning PBS Documentary* (2009)

PODCASTS

- *Grammar Girl: Quick and Dirty Tips* ™ by Mignon Fogarty
- *A Way with Words* by Martha Barnette and Grant Barrett
- *Faster Than Normal* by Peter Shankman
- Merriam Webster *Word of the Day*

WEBSITES

- *Wordsmith.org: The Magic of Words*
- *Richard Lederer's Verbivore*

Grantus Crowellius Maximus, Great Grantasmo, Social Word Chef, Tipper of Sacred Cows, Twisted Ice-Crusher, Shit Maker-Upper, and Best Morning Coffee Maker

Born and raised in Honolulu, Hawai'i, with a long adult-ing in the Chicago burbs, Grant now lives in Durham, North Carolina with his "spousish" partner, Karen.

A man wearing many hats, Grant is a virtual event coordinator for a global enterprise, a three-time social media manager on both the agency and brand side, a past YouTube channel manager for Fortune 100 enterprises, a nationwide conference speaker on video marketing, a former professional editorial cartoonist and talk radio host, a comedy club staffer, and a dabbler in documentary film production. He is a proud fighter of free speech for everyone, and was represented by the ACLU during his college years.

When he's not making up silly words, Grant is a guest speaker on being confident on camera, and on the unique relationship between social media and ADHD. (Fun note: while writing this book, he worked part-time as a Social media manager and video producer for a local jewelry business, where he was continuously surrounded by highly distractible, shiny objects—and jewelry, too.)

Grant also volunteers with Karen as foster parents for a cat and kitten adoption and rescue organization. For fun, he enjoys running in thousand-acre forest preserves, looking for the best craft beer deals across state lines, listening to offbeat podcasts, enjoying quirky documentaries, open mic nights, and getting into spirited dialog with humor.

His first solo book, *GRANTASMS!*, is the culmination of many years of word creations from his big ideas, small wonders, and unfinished business. He is an enthusiastic student of creative psychology and social health, and he explores twisted ways of treating people online with empathy daily. He succeeds some of the time, laughs at the others, gets pissy about a few, and tries to learn from them all.

Want to contact Grant? Speaking, consulting inquiries, interview guest, feedback on this book, or sharing a twisted word of your own? Care for a mint?

grant@yourtwistedwords.com

f facebook.com/yourtwistedwords

🐦 twitter.com/yurtwistedwords

📷 instagram.com/yourtwistedwords

Acknowledgements

Writing this book has been so much hard work.

So…much…hard…work.

I asked one of the interviewees in this book, Ann Handley, what her experience was like when she wrote her first book. She said, "it was like giving birth to a Honda Civic."

I think my experience was closer to a Honda SUV (the car Karen drives.) To all who helped make this a reality and have been so patient with me, I am profoundly grateful.

Thanks to my editors, Peter Heyrman and Alice Osborn, for giving me masterful direction and guidance for transforming my manuscript into a top-notch book, along with how to make it read much more clearly for a broader audience. I first met Alice at a local Meetup Book Club she organized in Raleigh, and then got to share her own author's story on the YouTube channel of an online book publishing platform I used to work for. As for Peter, I met him on Craigslist. (Professionally, people.)

Thanks to all of my beta readers and reviewers: Lisa Joy Tomey, Christine Crandell, Ginger Gorrell, Amy Crosby, Melissa Heisler, CJ Summers, Justin Landwehr, Alexis Nicole; and my sister, Tracy. They all helped me narrow down my hundreds of made-up words into this select set you see here in this book. (They also had to wade through a lot of the first draft that probably made them shake their heads, too.)

To my Human2Human (H2H) Marketing Club business coaching group led by Bryan and Courtney-Smith Kramer, filled with so many genuinely word-nerdy human beings. A big shout out to Lynn-Abate Johnson for her amazing enthusiasm and support, and also to authors Lyz Kelley and Chrissy Bernal for guiding me along professionally. I highly recommend checking out the group and becoming a member. Their support and direction with so many iterations of this book has been invaluable to me.

Thanks also to my ADHD community of supporters. Just to name a few: Gina Pera, Adult ADHD author, and journalist, for being my very first "volunteer" editor; David Giwerc, for being my very first ADHD professional "beta tester." To my Canadian neighbors—Rick and Ava Green for their profound inspiration and comedy that motivated me to actually learn more about ADHD, and have loads of fun doing it. A huge thank you as well to the mother-son team of Diane and DJ Charewicz for their many years of friendship and support with this project, including producing the video series and pre-cursor to this book, "What's Your Social Beef?" and "ADHD Dudes in Coffee Shops Goin' a Little Crazy."

Nani and Richard Crowell (aka "Mom & Dad"), thank you for having sex with each other and tolerating each other long enough to have me, and enduring me long enough to see some really positive things happen in my life. Raising me was way more work than with a regular kid, and hopefully, more interesting results. You're gone from this earth but never forgotten. Seriously, I love you both.

And most of all, I dedicate this book to the love of my life, Karen. This book just would not have been completed without her support. She has immense patience, understanding, insight, and a sense of humor that's as crass and creative as mine. She has persevered with reading and re-reading my drafts of this for years (yes, years), and her editing advice made it better and better until it was ready for the world.

Karen, you came to me during a very rough patch in my life nearly ten years ago. You gave me tough love and helped make me into the partner I needed to be. You had to endure my many verbal ideas and changes in my thinking—far too many times to count. Thank you for being proud of me, I love you so very much. This book is a small token of my gratitude, and you gave me an original word for our extraordinary beautiful and quirky relationship...

The Very End-notes

WORDS AT PLAY! GRANTASMS FOR EVERYDAY

Dana Winston Keller website http://www.danakeller.net/

GIMMEE MONEY! GRANTASMS FOR WORK

Grant Crowell YouTube channel http://www. youtube.com/grantast

YAY FOR FOOD! GRANTASMS FOR EATS

Instagram account @wecannoteven https://www.instagram. com/p/BSoIJAwgSn3

"Wafalafel: Delcious Blend-Free Waffled Falafels" https:// www.instructables.com/id/Wafalafel-Delicious-Blend-free-Waffled-Falafels/

DIGITAL DOUCHES! GRANTASMS FOR INTERWEBZ

Grant Crowell, "Digital Natives Transforming Online Video, Part 2: Training Digital Citizens," July 29, 2011 https:// tubularinsights.com/digital-natives-online-video/

SUPER SOCIALIZE ME! GRANTASMS FOR GERKS

Super Socialize ME! YouTube channel playlist https://www. youtube.com/playlist?list=PL7YYIm1EL99D84nbx-ipGj-ioqco8DN8t

Fred Nickols & Harvey Bergholz, "What's the Return on You

(ROY)?" Distance Consulting LLC (©2009) https://nickols.us~nickols1/roy.pdf

Bryan Kramer, "The Difference Between Solitude and Isolation." BryanKramer.com, November 29, 2018 https://www.bryankramer.com/the-difference-between-solitude-and-isolation

READY, PLAY, GRANTASMS!

Dr. Jennifer Lynne Bird, "Constantly Connected: Managing Stress in Today's Technological Times." *Human Development in the Digital Age,* ©2018 https://www.igi-global.com/chapter/constantly-connected/186226

Brené Brown, "The Power of Vulnerability," filmed June 2010, TEDx Houston https://www.ted.com/talks/brene_brown_on_vulnerability

WHO'S GOT A GRANTASM? THESE FOLKS!

Brandon Telig, "The Vulnerability of Storytelling," SelfNarate.com November 9, 2015 https://www.selfnarrate.com/resources/2015/10/1/the-vulnerability-of-storytelling

Chris Brogan, "10 Years After Trust Agents," ChrisBrogan.com website, June 22, 2019 https://chrisbrogan.com/trustagents10years/

"Definition of 'preunion,'" *Collins English Dictionary,* Accessed August 23, 2018 https://www.collinsdictionary.com/us/dictionary/english/preunion

MY TWISTED ADHD STORY

Grant Crowell, "Emotional Intelligence for Dummies: Pause is Power!," July 31, 2015 https://www.linkedin.com/pulse/emotional-intelligence-dummies-pause-power-grant-crowell/

NOTSPERTS: CHALLENGE EXPERTATIONS!

Grant Crowell, "'NotSperts vs. Real Social Media Experts!," November 23, 2016 https://www.linkedin.com/pulse/how-tell-real-social-media-expert-from-notspert-linkedin-crowell/

A

B

I JUST HAD A GRANTASM!

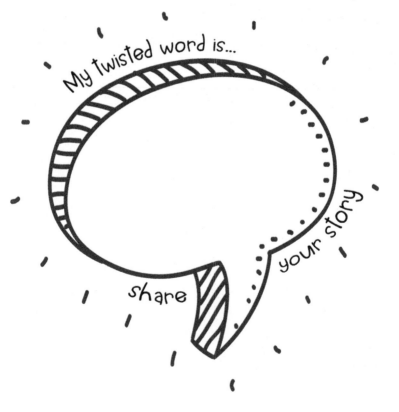

My twisted word is...

share your story

I JUST HAD A GRANTASM!

My twisted word is...

...share your story.

Made in the USA
Middletown, DE
06 July 2021